World Music

by Steve Waters

World Première Production
The Crucible, Sheffield
May 2003

World Music

By Steve Waters

Director	Josie Rourke
Designer	Christopher Oram
Lighting Designer	Neil Austin
Casting	Amy Ball
Assistant Designer	Paul Wills
Stage Manager	Sandra Blue
Deputy Stage Manager	Donna Reeves
Assistant Stage Manager	Kim Lewis
Production Photographer	Manuel Harlen

World Music

By Steve Waters

Cast in order of speaking:

Geoff Fallon	Nigel Lindsay
Tim Fallon/Young Geoff	Paul Ready
Paulette James	Sara Powell
Alan Carswell	Sebastian Harcombe
Jean Kiyabe	Nonso Anozie
Odette	Assly Zandry
Florence	Nikki Amuka-Bird

STEVE WATERS

Writer

Theatre: English Journeys (Hampstead 1998 (to be revived by Weaver-Hughes Theatre Company for Edinburgh 2003)); After the Gods (Hampstead 2002 (published by Faber)); translated Philippe Minyana's Habitats for RNT Studio staged at The Gate, London 2002 (published by Oberon); The Cull (Menagerie Theatre Company 2002, East Anglian tour).

Television: Safe House (BBC4, 2002).

Radio: The Moderniser (Radio 4, 2001).

Steve was Pearson TV Resident Dramatist at Hampstead Theatre 1999-2000 and is currently on attachment to the RNT Studio.

NIKKI AMUKA-BIRD
Florence

Training: LAMDA.

Theatre: RSC: Clarice in A Servant of Two Masters, Miranda in The Tempest, Helena in A Midsummer Night's Dream; Kitty/Shona in Top Girls and Tetley in 50 Revolutions (Oxford Stage Company). Nikki was Director/Choreographer and played Macbeth in Pidgin Macbeth for Ken Campbell.

Television: Martha in Grafters, Carole in Safe as Houses, Forgive and Forget (Granada); Constance in Man of Laws Tale - Canterbury Tales, Josie in Holby City, June in NCS Manhunt (BBC).

NONSO ANOZIE
Jean Kiyabe

Training: The Central School of Speech and Drama.

Theatre: King Lear in King Lear (RSC Academy, Ian Charleson Award, commendation); Mr Moses in White Folks (Tricycle Theatre) and Marcus in The Box (Cockpit Theatre/Talawa).

Television: Singer in Nights Out At The Empire (Channel 4).

SEBASTIAN HARCOMBE
Alan Carswell

Training: RADA. Winner of the Robert Donat Prize.

Theatre: Marcel Proust in Remembrance of Things Past (European Critics Circle nomination - Best Actor), Aegisthus in The Oresteia, Marchbanks in Candida (RNT); Arthur in Early Morning and the title role in Frankenstein (RNT Studio); Malcolm in Macbeth, Clitandre in The Learned Ladies, Oliver in As You Like It (RSC); Mercutio in Romeo & Juliet and Flamineo in The White Devil (Lyric Hammersmith); The Woman in Black (West End); Peter Quilpe in The Cocktail Party (Edinburgh Festival - 50th Anniversary Production); Calisto in La Celestina (ATC); Young Tantalus/The Fury in Thyestes (Royal Court) and Malcolm in Macbeth (Crucible, Sheffield).

Television: Prince Felix Yussupov in The Soviets.

Radio: Boris in The Roads to Freedom and Alyosha in The Brothers Karamatzov.

Film: Carrington and the forthcoming Swimming Pool of Francois Ozon.

NIGEL LINDSAY
Geoff Fallon

Training: Webber Douglas Academy - awarded the Amherst Webber Scholarship.

Theatre: Stephano in The Tempest (Old Vic); Nick in Bedroom Farce (Aldwych); Push Up (Royal Court); Max in The Real Thing (Donmar Warehouse/Albery West End/Ethel Barrymore Theater, New York); Morphic Resonance (Donmar Warehouse); London Cuckolds and Blue Remembered Hills (RNT); The Tower (Almeida); Mugsy in Dealer's Choice (Vaudeville /RNT); Katerina (Lyric Hammersmith); Hamlet (Crucible, Sheffield); King Lear (Royal Court); Relative Values (Salisbury Playhouse); Anna Karenina (Shared Experience); The Girl Who Fell To Earth (Great Eastern Stage).

Television: My Family, Midsomer Murders; I'm Alan Partridge, The Armando Iannucci Show; Brass Eye; Too Much Sun (series); Deja vu (Channel 4 Shockers); Harbour Lights; A Dance to The Music of Time; Dressing for Breakfast (series 1 - 3); A Few Short Journeys of the Heart; The Bill; Between the Lines; Bye Bye Baby.

Film: Blackball; Mike Bassett: England Manager; Rogue Trader.

Radio: Frederick in Frederick & Augusta; People Like Us; Morphic Resonance; Crossing the Equator.

SARA POWELL
Paulette James

Theatre: Stella Marr in Racing Demon, Mary Housego in Absence of War and Irina Platt in Murmuring Judges (Birmingham Rep); Nadia in Mapping the Edge (Crucible, Sheffield); Cariola in The Duchess of Malfi (RSC); Mardell in The Villain's Opera, Maureen in Honk, Scylla in Darker Face of the Earth and Adromanche in Troilus and Cressida (RNT); Lady Lucy in The Bassett Table (Wild Iris Co); Dorcas Ableman in Golden Girls (Mercury, Colchester); Dabby in Our Country's Good (Theatr Clwyd); Royal Court Young Writers Festival (Royal Court); Magdalena in The House of Bernarda Alba (The Brix Theatre).

Television: Dinotopia (Hallmark); Silent Witness, Holby City, Doctors, EastEnders, Vanity Fair, Casualty, Murder Most Horrid,

Between the Lines (BBC); The Bill (Thames); Desmond's (Humphrey Barclay Prod); Rumble (Bentley Prod); Tales from a Darkened Room - The Confessions of Arthur Crewinman (Capital Films/Channel 4); London's Burning (2 series) (LWT).

PAUL READY
Tim/Young Geoff

Training: LAMDA.

Theatre: Terrorism, Crazyblackmuthafuckin'self (Royal Court); Romeo & Juliet and Twelfth Night (Liverpool Playhouse); Mother Clapp's Molly House (RNT); Cuckoos (Gate Theatre); The Beggar's Opera (Wilton's Music Hall).

Television: Jeffrey Archer - The Truth (Hattrick/BBC); Heartbeat (YTV); Tipping the Velvet and Chambers (BBC); Harry Enfield Presents (Tiger Aspect/BBC).

Film: Maybe Baby; Angels and Insects.

ASSLY ZANDRY
Odette

Training: BA Hons Performing Arts, Middlesex University (1997-2000).

Theatre: Stage debut as Elmire in an adaptation of Molière's Tartuffe in France. Roles in England include: the musical Sweeney Todd; the Greek tragedy Blood Lust and lead vocalist in Cabaret: the Pervert Lounge.

Television: Jackie in As If (Channel 4); Bad Girls; Waking the Dead (BBC) and Emma Brody (US television).

Extra: Assly can speak four languages and has taught African Dance.

JOSIE ROURKE
Director

Theatre: Josie Rourke trained at the Donmar Warehouse, where she was assistant director to Michael Grandage, Nicholas Hytner, Phyllida Lloyd and Sam Mendes. She then worked as assistant director to Peter Gill at the RNT and for English Touring Theatre.

Directing credits include: Frame 312 (Donmar Warehouse); Kick For Touch (Peter Gill Festival, Crucible Studio, Sheffield); Romeo & Juliet (Liverpool Playhouse); Crazyblackmuthafuckin'self and Children's Day (Royal Court).

Josie has a year-long bursary at the Royal Court to train as an associate director.

CHRISTOPHER ORAM
Designer

For the Crucible: The Tempest, Richard III, Don Juan, Edward II, The Country Wife, Six Degrees of Separation, As You Like It, Twelfth Night and What The Butler Saw.

Other recent credits include: Caligula, The Vortex, Privates on Parade, Merrily We Roll Along, Passion Play and Good (Donmar Warehouse); Fucking Games (Royal Court, Upstairs); The Marriage Play/Finding The Sun and Summerfolk (RNT); Dinner With Friends (Hampstead); The Jew of Malta (Almeida); Aristocrats and The Eccentricities of a Nightingale (Gate, Dublin and New York); A Streetcar Named Desire (Bristol Old Vic); Twelfth Night (Royal Dramatic Theatre, Sweden) and The Embalmer (Almeida).

Future work includes: Power (RNT) and A Midsummer Night's Dream (Crucible, Sheffield).

NEIL AUSTIN
Lighting Designer

Theatre: Previously with Josie Rourke: Romeo and Juliet (Liverpool Playhouse); previously with Christopher Oram: Caligula (Donmar Warehouse); The Embalmer (Almeida Opera).

Other Theatre Credits include: A Prayer for Owen Meany, The Walls and Further than the Furthest Thing (RNT); Japes (Theatre Royal, Haymarket, West End); Flesh Wound and Trust (Royal Court); Monkey (Young Vic); American Buffalo (Royal Exchange, Manchester); The Lady in the Van and Pretending to be Me (West Yorkshire Playhouse); Great Expectations (Bristol Old Vic); King Hedley II (Birmingham Rep & Tricycle); Mr Placebo (Traverse, Edinburgh and Drum, Plymouth); Loves Work, Cuckoos, Venecia, Marathon and Une Tempete (Gate Theatre); Closer (Teatro Broadway, Buenos Aires).

Musical Credits include: Babes in Arms (International Festival of Musical Theatre); Spend, Spend, Spend (UK Tour (co-design with Mark Henderson)); Rags (Guildhall); Cabaret (MacOwan Theatre); My Fair Lady (Teatro Nacional, Buenos Aires).

Opera Credits Include: Orfeo (Opera City, Tokyo and Japanese Tour); Pulse Shadows (Queen Elizabeth Hall); L'Enfant Prodigue,

The Peter Gill festival, Crucible Studio
Peter Brook Empty Space Award Winner 2002

Best Musical, High Society
Barclays TMA Regional Theatre Awards
(nomination)

Theatre of the Year 2001
Barclays TMA Regional Theatre Awards

Best Actress, Victoria Hamilton, As You Like It
Barclays TMA Regional Theatre Awards

Best Director, Michael Grandage, As You Like It
Evening Standard Theatre Awards

Best Director, Michael Grandage, As You Like It
The Critic's Circle Award

As You Like It
The South Bank Show Award for Theatre

Financial Times/Arts & Business Awards
(shortlisted)

Victoria Hamilton in
As You Like It
2000

Photograph: Simon Warner

Joseph Fiennes in
Edward II
2001

Photograph: Ivan Kyncl

Matt Bardock and
Justin Salinger in
Kick for Touch
2002

Photograph: Simon Annand

Sheffield Theatres is the largest theatre complex outside London, offering a wide range of performances from drama to dance, comedy to musicals.

The Crucible Theatre, built in 1971 houses a thrust stage and is the main producing venue in the complex. Recently awarded the Barclays Theatre of the Year Award, productions have included a new version of Iphigenia by Edna O'Brien and Amanda Donohoe in Teeth 'n' Smiles, both directed by Anna Mackmin, Philip Pullman's work on stage for the first time in Stephen Russell's adaptation of The Firework-Maker's Daughter directed by Paul Hunter and Hayley Carmichael, Sweet Charity directed by Timothy Sheader, and Derek Jacobi in The Tempest, Kenneth Branagh in Richard III, Tom Hollander in Don Juan, Joseph Fiennes in Edward II and Victoria Hamilton in As You Like It, all directed by Sheffield Theatres' Associate Director Michael Grandage.

The Lyceum Theatre, built in 1897, receives the country's top touring productions including visits by the National Theatre, The Royal Shakespeare Company, Opera North, Northern Ballet Theatre and hit shows from the West End.

The Studio Theatre is a flexible 'black box' space playing host to smaller touring companies, contemporary dance and the world famous Lindsays and Friends Chamber Music Festivals. Recently awarded the Peter Brook Empty Space Award, Sheffield Theatres productions in the Studio have included Could It Be Magic? (with Unlimited Theatre), Macbeth adapted and directed by James Phillips and the Peter Gill Festival.

Kenneth Branagh in
Richard III
2002

Derek Jacobi in
The Tempest
2002

Amanda Donohoe in
Teeth 'n' Smiles
2002

Photographs: Ivan Kyncl

Sheffield Theatres operates a flexible membership scheme that not only rewards frequent theatre goers but also encourages young first-time attenders. Benefits include:

- A range of membership levels to suit every need and budget
- Generous ticket discounts
- Priority booking
- Talks, tours and opportunities to meet the acting companies and production teams
- Regular newsletter and brochure mailings
- Members' Hotline

For further information contact Alison Moore:
Tel: 0114 249 6007/email: a.moore@sheffieldtheatres.co.uk

Sheffield Theatres Education Programme actively engages people in the work of the theatre through a varied and challenging programme of activities and events. It is designed for all those who wish to understand and discover more about the process of creating theatre. The Education Programme reflects the rich cultural diversity of its community and encourages access and inclusion. It includes:

- Theatre in schools and community venues
- Youth theatre and projects with young people
- Special education projects with the early years, schools and colleges, and the community
- Education Programmes supporting Sheffield Theatres productions including talks, a range of workshops, and resource packs
- Backstage tours and specialist tours
- Work experience and student placements
- Training and development programmes for teachers and education workers

For further information contact Sue Burley, Education Administrator on 0114 249 5999 or visit www.sheffieldtheatres.co.uk/education.

**Sheffield
Assay Office**

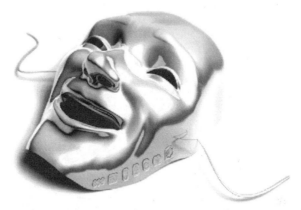

There's no drama
with British Hallmarks

THE BRITISH HALLMARK - PROTECTING THE CONSUMER FOR OVER 700 YEARS

British Hallmarking dates back 700 years and represents the earliest form of consumer protection. The Hallmark shows that precious metal articles have been independently tested by an Assay Office and guarantees that the article conforms to a specified legal standard of purity. The Hallmark consists of three compulsory symbols: a sponsor's mark, the fineness number and the Assay Office mark. Unless specifically exempted, all gold, silver and platinum articles offered for sale must be Hallmarked. There may be additional voluntary marks, *eg* a date letter, a fineness symbol, a common control mark. The Hallmarking Act permits other European Area Hallmarks and standards of fineness.

Sponsor *The registered mark of the maker or sponsor of the piece*	Millesimal Number *Indicates the precious metal content. The shape of the shield identifies the metal as gold, silver or platinum*	Assay Office *The mark of the Assay Office where the piece was tested*	Fineness Symbol *A traditional symbol denoting one of the older precious metal finenesses*	Date Letter *A letter representing the year in which the piece was hallmarked*	Common Control Mark *Indicates countries which are signatories to the International Convention on Hallmarking*

Assay Master: Ashley Carson, PO Box 187, 137 Portobello Street, Sheffield, S1 4DS
Tel: 0114 275 5111 Fax: 0114 275 6473
carsona@assayoffice.co.uk

WORLD MUSIC

Steve Waters

*'How much blood there is in my memory.
In my memory are lagoons.'*

Aimé Césaire, *Cahier d'un retour au pays natal*

*'The Explorer thought to himself: It's always
a ticklish matter to intervene decisively
in other people's affairs'*

Franz Kafka, *In the Penal Colony*

Acknowledgements

The author would like to thank Mary Kayetsi Blewitt and Richard Howitt, MEP, for their assistance in the researching of this play, which is dedicated to SURF (Survivor's Fund), an organisation which seeks to support those surviving the 1994 Rwandan genocide.

Author's Note

Irundi and its history is a fiction, as are actions of the European politicans in the play; nevertheless this fiction is not allegorical, and is closely related to the tragic histories of Rwanda and Burundi.

Characters

GEOFF FALLON, *mid-forties MEP; then as a man in his early twenties played by the same actor who plays:*

TIM FALLON, *nineteen-year-old son of Geoff*

PAULETTE JAMES, *Labour MEP, Afro-Carribean, late forties*

ALAN CARSWELL, *MEP, Chair of Socialist group, late thirties*

JEAN KIYABE, *twenty-six-year-old Bourgmestre (communal leader) in Irundi, then émigré in early forties*

ODETTE, *twenty-six-year-old housemaid to Kiyabe*

FLORENCE, *twenty-five-year-old Irundi refugee*

Settings

Brussels, the immediate present and recent past

Geoff's flat; the canteen, bar and offices in the European Parliament Building; the European Parliament Chamber of Deputies; Bruxelles-Midi train station.

Irundi in 1980

The porch of Jean Kiyabe's partially-constructed house.

ONE: EUROPE

The following scenes play continuously in the same space:

A GEOFF, TIM *and* FLORENCE, *Café, Bruxelles Midi-station, the present, March.*

B GEOFF, ALAN *and* PAULETTE, *European Parliament bar, Brussels, the previous June.*

C GEOFF, PAULETTE *and* JEAN, *European Parliament buildings and Conference Chamber, the previous July.*

D JEAN *speaking in European Parliament Conference Chamber, previous July, a day later.*

E GEOFF *giving a talk to schoolchildren several years earlier.*

A *March, the present:Bruxelles-Midi Café, late.* TIM *with rucksack at standing table with* GEOFF, FLORENCE *in background.*

GEOFF (*embracing him*). Welcome to Europe.

TIM. Jesus, dad.

GEOFF. Well.

B *Previous June; European Parliament:*ALAN *on bar-stool with* GEOFF *and* PAULETTE.

ALAN. Welcome to Europe. As it were.

GEOFF. So this is Europe. I thought it was Belgium.

PAULETTE. As good a place to start as any.

They laugh.

C *Previous July; Lobby of European Parliament building.*

GEOFF. Bienvenue à Europe.

PAULETTE. You'll have to put up with our appalling French.

JEAN. It's good, good French. Ça marche.

GEOFF. Better than my Kirundi.

JEAN. No Geoffrey no you are too modest.

PAULETTE. Ah, 'Geoffrey'.

She laughs.

GEOFF. Geoff, please, Jean. There was never anyone called Geoffrey.

A *Bruxelles-Midi Café:* TIM *folds out map at table.*

TIM. Overnight to Oslo. Breakfast in Copenhagen. Eight hours in Amsterdam.

GEOFF. Lay off the wacky baccy.

TIM. Advice of an old hand.

GEOFF. Lay off the drugs and the sex-workers.

TIM. Says prominent MEP. Behave dad.

GEOFF. Less of the prominent.

TIM. We're doing the camps. Dachau. Buchenwald. And Eurodisney, which'll be wicked.

FLORENCE *approaches.*

FLORENCE. Qu'est-que vous voulez, messieurs?

GEOFF. Go on then. Dazzle us with your linguistic mastery.

TIM. She'll know English.

GEOFF. Not the point. You're not in bloody England.

TIM. Err – Je veux – nous voulons –

FLORENCE. Oui?

TIM. They don't do B. L. T.

FLORENCE. Pardon.

GEOFF. Deux pressions et deux…deux baguettes avec fromage.

TIM. Yeah. Merci. God I'm starved.

FLORENCE. Bon.

GEOFF. Vous avez 'Primus'?

FLORENCE. Ah oui. Et Stella.

GEOFF. Primus. Ça, c'est mon fils.

He embraces TIM.

TIM. Lay off. He's drunk.

GEOFF. No. I'm not.

FLORENCE. Ah. D'accord.

She goes.

TIM. I can't stick about. Took ages getting through Kent. Snow. First snow in ages. Meeting Maeve and Becky at the hostel. They lock you out after one.

GEOFF. I'll walk you there.

TIM. This time of night? Get a knife in us.

GEOFF. No no I often walk here. Walked here tonight.

TIM. Why?

GEOFF. Few things to think about. Girlfriends? Becky and Maeve?

TIM. No, no, just mates. You look…different.

C *In the lobby of the European Parliament (July).*

JEAN. You haven't changed my friend.

GEOFF. No you really haven't changed. I have.

PAULETTE. I think Geoff's filled out actually.

GEOFF. He won't get that.

PAULETTE. Geoffrey est plus grande.

JEAN. Oui. Bon santé.

   JEAN *hugs him.*

GEOFF. Oh you've lost weight.

JEAN. A little.

GEOFF. Your clothes hang on you.

JEAN. Hungry times.

PAULETTE. Of course.

GEOFF. We forget this too easy. This aspect of it.

JEAN. You are too far, too far from us.

A *Bruxelles-Midi, present;* FLORENCE *serves the baguettes.*

TIM. Look a bit stale.

GEOFF. It's midnight. You don't get fresh bread at midnight.

   FLORENCE *serves the beer.*

   These people work while the city sleeps. Crawl back to
   some bleak hole in Ixelles. Stale bread'll do us.

   They eat; FLORENCE *murmurs a tune.*

   How's…your mother?

TIM. Oh. Fine. Y'know, fine.

GEOFF. Good. Good. Still alone?

TIM. Why do you ask?

   GEOFF *shrugs.*

GEOFF. Sometimes wonder what you say about me.

TIM. Don't bother. (*He laughs.*) Her idea, this. That we should
   meet.

GEOFF. OK.

TIM. You haven't got a coat, dad. Must be cold.

GEOFF. Don't notice the cold, me.

FLORENCE *plays a tape of African music.*

GEOFF. Listen. Listen to that. Yeah?

TIM. African.

GEOFF. Real music, that. Turn it up. Plus volume.

TIM. Never been much into world music stuff.

GEOFF *looks at* FLORENCE; *she looks back.*

GEOFF. She's eyeing us up.

TIM. Don't stare.

GEOFF. Tall. Must be my height.

TIM. Stop staring at her.

GEOFF. She's looking at me. That's the code. She's not coy like us.

TIM. Well I'm not some big African expert like you.

GEOFF. C'est très très bon, la musique.

FLORENCE. Yes. From my country.

TIM. Shit. She understood us. She understood all the things we said.

GEOFF. Ah, you speak English mademoiselle?

TIM. All that crap you came out with.

FLORENCE. Of course. This is Europe.

GEOFF. Will you join us?

TIM. I've got to get to the hostel.

FLORENCE. It's late. I am closing. I am very tired, sirs.

C *Lobby of European Parliament (July).*

PAULETTE. How do you like Brussels?

JEAN. An extraordinary city. A real city. Incredible size
    buildings, light. All the light, even at night.

GEOFF. I got a car, a bloody BMW. Drove him straight from
    the airport. EU chauffeur.

JEAN. I have of course often read about this city. But in reality
    it is finer and also dirtier.

GEOFF. Met him at the airport. You know with one of those
    signs. 'Monsieur Kiyabe'.

JEAN (*laughs*). You looked like an airhostess, truly. It was
    kind of you. I was very confused, I am confused in airports.
    I have little experience of them.

PAULETTE. Must have been difficult. Getting out of your
    country.

JEAN. I have no country madame.

GEOFF. Jean's been in the Congo. Got a UN transport to
    Uganda.

PAULETTE. So you're formally in exile, then.

JEAN. Here, there. It is the same.

PAULETTE. I'm sorry I'm being obtuse.

JEAN. You will have seen the pictures perhaps.

GEOFF. Whole community, upsticks.

PAULETTE. Yes, we've seen terrible images, heard terrible
    things.

GEOFF. We don't know the half of it.

E *Coventry, some years earlier;* GEOFF *talking to schoolchildren; he sshhhes them.*

GEOFF. OK. This is the village where I stayed. That's the
    lake, just down from the village, in an old volcano. You'll

have looked at Volcanos in Geography. There are many
lakes and mountains in this area which might surprise those
of you who think Africa's all desert. The picture's a bit
blurred because my lens got steamed up. Can you see the
swimmers there in the lake?

Sound of a class of children intoning 'Yes'.

The whole village swam in this lake.

Faint sound of laughter, splashing.

D *A conference chamber in the European Parliament, July,
following day; Jean sweats and blinks in the glare of light.*

JEAN. 'The International Community'. I cannot say that
I understand this phrase. I cannot say that I believe in such
an idea. If there is an International Community then I think
I must say it has failed us in our struggles. The United
Nations stands back from our war. The Aid community too,
stands by, or worse, takes sides, yes. Some of my people
say, 'Europe, they take what they want and then they go'.
The old know it, the young people; 'Europe is one great
hungry bird, eating us, eating our work, our lives, our
people': they remember that you came to us all of you and
what you took again and again: the German people; the
Englishmen; the Belgians and the French. They have died in
your fields to grow the tea you drink, the coffee you grind
and roast, the beer in your bottles, they have died and you
have built cities on their bones and you have forgotten this
you have forgotten all of this. Ah forgive me, forgive me.
(*He pauses, breathes.*) I am very sorry for my anger. I am
here in sadness not anger.

B *Bar in the European Parliament (June).*

ALAN. Let's get some drinks in; oil the cogs. Beer Geoff?

GEOFF. Sure.

PAULETTE. You always drank stout.

ALAN. Stout? Does it still exist?

GEOFF. I drink all sorts. I'll have a mild if they have it.

PAULETTE. And he smoked rollies.

ALAN. Good Old Left vices.

GEOFF. Less of the 'Old' please. I even drink the odd cappuccino from time to time. I'll get them...

ALAN. No no. My shout. Then we'll take a look at the communication.

GEOFF. What?

PAULETTE. Your speech. To the plenary.

GEOFF. You've read it?

ALAN. Of course.

PAULETTE. You need Alan's approval.

ALAN. Well it's not formally necessary.

PAULETTE. Not formally no. But if I'm going to nominate you it needs to be kosher.

GEOFF. OK. Well if that's how it works, fine. So let's talk –

ALAN. They won't have mild. They have Guinness.

PAULETTE. I'll go for a Stella.

GEOFF. I'm also drafting a report. I'll convene a round-table and bring some of the key players over from Africa, from Irundi and neighbouring states; Alan, you could call an extraordinary meeting of the Socialist group, sidelining the French –

ALAN. Geoff, du calme, du calme; let's sort the drinks out.

GEOFF. Sure, sorry. Paulette and I used to move pretty fast on such matters. She's probably told you –

PAULETTE. The less said about West Midland politics the better –

GEOFF. We went head on, we bounced stuff; direct action, really.

PAULETTE. We were very young then.

ALAN. Paulette's very highly thought of.

PAULETTE. More strategic these days, perhaps.

GEOFF. I'll believe it when I see it. You had fire in you.

ALAN. Politics can't feed off fire alone.

GEOFF. I'm not here for politics.

ALAN. It's a matter of craft Geoff. Keeping something back, right? So. Guinness, Stella, Hoechbier.

He goes.

PAULETTE. You're forcing the pace. Chill out a bit.

She adjusts his tie.

GEOFF. He's going to trash it. Wanker.

PAULETTE. He's a good barometer of where the Party is. You need Alan on your side.

GEOFF. I know his sort. On the pager all day networkfucking.

PAULETTE. He gets things done. Which I respect. Pace yourself.

GEOFF. You know what Paulette I don't get any less impatient. With corridors and rooms off corridors and agendas and papers and briefings and sub-committee working parties and canvassing in old folk's homes and speaking shit in church-halls; but you know what: I'm here now. And so are you.

PAULETTE. There's plenty of corridors here Geoff.

GEOFF. Let's open some doors then. Let's open a load of windows.

A *Cafe Bruxelles-Midi station, the present.*

TIM. Is this what you do, dad? Cruise bars.

GEOFF. Cette musique est belle.

TIM. She speaks English.

GEOFF. Beautiful music. From Irundi?

She nods her head; lights a cigarette.

FLORENCE. I have to close.

GEOFF. You're a refugee, right.

She shrugs.

TIM. Dad.

GEOFF. Keeping your head down eh.

FLORENCE. Pardon?

GEOFF. Skivvying, in here, minimum rate, less than that. What do they pay you? Couple of Euros a day. If that.

FLORENCE. C'est l'argent.

She laughs.

TIM. You interested in me at all dad? I got four A levels. I've been working in Sainsbury's. Any of this of interest?

GEOFF. I'm sorry. I'm tired, Tim. Had a pretty bad day.

TIM. My mates gave me a party, a send off. I drank a whole bottle of ouzo.

GEOFF. What does he sing? In the song? Can't make it out.

FLORENCE. Monsieur?

GEOFF. Les mots de chanson.

TIM. Yeah I went out with Becky but now I fancy Maeve. I've got a deferred place to read Computing at Manchester.

FLORENCE. He sings about growing seeds.

TIM. None of this seems to mean much to you.

FLORENCE. You know err, sorghum. Planting sorghum grains.

GEOFF. Sorghum's a sort of millet, Tim. You get in this beer in fact. Staple product.

TIM. And you, you look so weird. Your suit's a mess. How can you do your job looking like that? I tell you I wouldn't vote for you.

TIM *gets up.*

GEOFF. Tim. Wait. Sit down.

TIM. No. No. I'm late I'm gonna be late.

GEOFF. Stop over.

TIM. I've booked it all I don't want to stop over.

GEOFF. Tim. I'm just tired. Hey, Tim. I need to talk to you.

TIM. You're rambling.

GEOFF. At the very least I've kept faith, right. With people.
I may have failed at many things – Tim, wait wait. You
make commitments, and I believe you must – abide by
them. Or else what are you, what are you, you're nothing.

C *European Parliament Conference Chamber (July), night.*

PAULETTE. So. The conference chamber. If I can find the
lights.

GEOFF. Looks even weirder in the dark.

JEAN. Ah. It feels very – big.

GEOFF. Got to cram a continent in here, mate.

JEAN. Like a great valley!

GEOFF. You'll be somewhere down there. The platform.

PAULETTE. It's designed to be non-hierarchical.

JEAN. There is nothing like this in our nation, in our
continent!

GEOFF. Nation shall speak unto nation.

PAULETTE. Lights!

JEAN. Ah.

They look.

GEOFF. There. In all its glory.

JEAN. Big enough for a village. (*Laughs.*)

GEOFF. Great acoustic. (*Shouts.*) Bonjour. Bongiorno. Guten Tag.

PAULETTE. We don't want to worry security.

GEOFF. You'll be up here, Alan Carswell centre chairing; guy from the Development committee; Portugese Minister. Your text piped through to each desk.

JEAN. How will they understand me?

PAULETTE. Simultaneous translation.

JEAN. A pentecost.

PAULETTE. Yes, yes, all speaking in tongues.

They laugh.

JEAN. What languages?

PAULETTE. English. I hope.

GEOFF. German.

PAULETTE. Portugese. Spanish.

GEOFF. Dutch.

JEAN. How will they understand me?

GEOFF. Swedish.

PAULETTE. Yes. Danish.

GEOFF. Finnish for fuck's sake.

JEAN. What is Finnish?

PAULETTE. Greek.

GEOFF. We said Dutch?

PAULETTE. Danish, Italian.

JEAN. How will they understand what I have come to say?

D *Following day, European Parliament, Conference Chamber.*

JEAN. I have many friends in Europe, I am here because of friends. I am very grateful to my friends who have stood by me. Church-leaders. Teachers. Engineers. Military advisors. Ah, you flow through my country friends, you, we call you birds – (*Laughs.*) 'Europeans': 'they who fly'; flying in with plans, plans for water retention, for water drainage, for pre-school education, plans for family planning – you have such plans for us, and we think: all will be changed, and promises are made, friendships formed, and then in our time of need, our struggle, away, you are gone again, gone, birds in the sky.

B *European Parliament, bar (June).*

ALAN. It's a fine speech. Stark. Terrifically persuasive.

GEOFF. Thank you. Thanks.

PAULETTE. It's the commitment.

ALAN. Very strong. And you've got good endorsements, Paulette amongst them. Impressively broad base of support.

GEOFF. I think it cuts beyond party this issue –

ALAN. I congratulate you on the power of the speech.

Pause.

GEOFF. I feel a 'but' coming on.

ALAN. May I be frank with you?

GEOFF. Of course.

ALAN. Good, good. I have a problem with the analysis.

PAULETTE. Perhaps Alan without the context, perhaps –

GEOFF. No go on. You were saying.

ALAN. I don't claim to have your Development expertise.

GEOFF. This is not simply about Development. It's about intercommunal slaughter.

ALAN. 'Slaughter' you say. Yes you use that word in here.

GEOFF. Yes. A good anglo-saxon word.

ALAN. I think the words we use on this issue are terribly important.

PAULETTE. Geoff's written a further communique on that very issue.

ALAN. You see this speech was so powerful that I felt I had to – show it to people I trust. Because frankly I felt you were wrong. I say I felt that.

PAULETTE. I don't think Alan you can question Geoff's expertise in this area. He has spent a great deal of time and committed an enormous amount of energy to Irundian life, politics.

GEOFF. On the ground.

ALAN. Yes, that's apparent. Your commitment is not in question. Well, no, perhaps it is. In question. Remind me again of the nature of your links with Irundi, Geoff.

GEOFF. Is this material?

PAULETTE. This is the context he perhaps lacks.

ALAN. Of course you don't have to tell me anything.

GEOFF. I went there as a student. With a church group in fact. Having dropped out of University in disgust. Wanting to *do* something, y'know.

ALAN. Admirable.

GEOFF. I don't know. Anyway I made contacts and I was determined to maintain those contacts and I swore one day I would bring what little influence I might have in my life, I don't know, in education I thought, then politics, to do what I could *here*, because, I felt, it was fine going out to Africa, having a Gap Year, getting laid and catching malaria and, fine, but what then, you see, after all the existential stuff – and the power as we know is in fact here, isn't it, not there. Enough context?

ALAN. I wonder if we don't set too much store by our own particular experiences.

GEOFF. I tell you what Alan I don't trust anything else, finally.

Pause.

PAULETTE. Geoff maintained contacts with numerous players in the state and civil society.

ALAN. I ran the speech past a couple of researchers active in charities based in the region –

GEOFF. Who? Which ones?

ALAN. That's not important. Well-placed NGOs.

GEOFF. I'm not liked by certain NGOs. Most NGOs.

PAULETTE. Actually Geoff I think you go too far here.

GEOFF. 'Cos I've seen how they operate, the Christian junkets, UN paycheque boys in their 4-wheel-drives, hose the blood off, then back to the barbecue in the compound –

ALAN. That's quite outrageous.

GEOFF. – swimming in the local water supplies.

ALAN. Nevertheless even in your own terms you'd have to acknowledge they have been 'on the ground' –

GEOFF. You want to censor my speech –

PAULETTE. I think you should at least hear Alan out.

ALAN. I'm not in the business of censoring anything.

GEOFF. I actually get pretty angry about this.

ALAN. That's apparent.

GEOFF. Do you get angry about things Alan?

ALAN. Returning to the speech. My colleagues also got pretty angry. I quote one at random: 'Having worked hard to get a recognition from the international community that we had a genocide of the Kanga people on our hands –'

GEOFF. Typically modish thinking. Bandying about terms such as genocide.

ALAN. So you say. Could you clarify that?

GEOFF. A word designed to shut down any nuanced political analysis –

PAULETTE. Geoff, actually, sorry Alan, but, Geoff, let's think about the impact your speech might have. The EU's considering pretty sizeable sums of emergency aid for the post-genocide, well post-war regime –

GEOFF. Yes yes, arm the victors, the ones who speak our language –

PAULETTE. Hang on – the country is in ruins, you acknowledge that.

GEOFF. The invasion has decimated a pretty underdeveloped infrastructure.

PAULETTE. I was talking about fatalities.

GEOFF. There are many dead, yes.

ALAN. Slaughtered I suppose. Presumably by someone.

PAULETTE. So if your speech has the desired effect, the Parliament will delay or even veto this money requested by the new regime; indeed may even make problematic EU recognition with all that flows from that – I just want to be clear about that –

GEOFF. The new regime is as racially motivated as the outgoing one. More so. You want context. OK. This is a country as we now all know with a combustible ethnic mix, the Muntu people in the majority, the Kanga people the minority. That's established, that we all agree on. But your NGOs and their media buddies need melodrama: they talk up 'tribes' and 'ancestral hatreds', they peddle a horror story in which suddenly, a month back, the Muntu majority go psycho and run amok with machetes, killing Kanga folk left, right and centre until their exiled brethren sweep in from abroad to expel the evil Muntu once and for all. New reign of light and reason. NGOs descend in droves. Demands for shitloads of Eurocash. This I presume is what your friends have been telling you, Alan?

ALAN. Well. In a crudely caricatured form, yes.

GEOFF. OK. Well it plays well in *The Guardian*. But it's unhistorical. It's sentimental. It's based on racist presuppositions. First off there's no tribes or separate genepools or hard and fast delineations in Irundi – yes, there are kin-groups, there are regional groups, there's that highly unfashionable thing, class; but the 'tribe' thing was cooked up and compounded by Europeans; nice convenient way to organise your native subjects into two groups and whip up as much hatred between them as possible, buoying up the richer minority who lord it over the Muntu masses and guarantee a nice little flow of raw materials and christian subjection.

ALAN. Geoff this is all fascinating stuff but I frankly don't see the relevance of –

GEOFF. The parents of those claimed to have been on a killing spree were slaves of Kanga lords within our lifetime; over the border brother and sister Muntu are slaughtered with impunity by a Kanga supremacist regime who we pay no heed to.

ALAN. You seem to be going out of your way to relativise documented acts of mass-murder.

GEOFF. The problem with us Alan is we forget about memory. We think Imperialism was in another time and life. The Belgians were there forty, not even forty years ago. Forty years ago the Muntu people were serfs in a medieval Belgian backed slave-state. Where were you forty years ago?

ALAN. I'm happy to say I wasn't around forty –

GEOFF. Well, OK, your family? The lives of your family?

ALAN. Oh, come on Geoff, it was an entirely different world.

GEOFF. We carry it with us Alan. The legacies. Within the span of one life, nothing fundamentally changes, I mean we're still fighting the battles of our parents – Paulette'll tell you she can't walk into certain constituency pubs and guarantee her own safety –

PAULETTE. Geoff, don't invoke me here –

GEOFF. – we're talking about victims killing victims. A hard truth perhaps. Unpalatable to your friends in the NGOs who need it nice and simple to keep up the cashflow.

ALAN. I take exception to this cynicism. I trust these people.

GEOFF. I trust conditions. I trust memory. I have been in a village where Muntu and Kanga folk lived alongside each other; I saw not one iota of evidence in all my time there to suggest the capacity for the sort of calculated wholesale violence that we are now being asked to accept. I saw a people growing crops in depleted soil, struggling to achieve literacy, a people trying to build a nation from the ruins of the real genocide, the one we are *all* culpable of. I start from my belief in these people not your people and their *analyses*.

Silence. They drink.

ALAN. Leave us for a bit Geoff, if you don't mind.

GEOFF. OK. I can…I mean there's more –

ALAN. Get another round in or something. Orange juice for me. Got a delegacy from the Baltic states in five minutes.

GEOFF. Sure. Sure. Orange juice.

PAULETTE. Same for me.

ALAN nods. GEOFF gets up.

GEOFF. I can supply all sorts of further documentation to –

PAULETTE. We need to talk Geoff.

GEOFF. Orange juice all round then.

He goes; ALAN leafs through the speech.

ALAN. He's good. Knows the terrain. To be honest I'm not up to speed on this one. I mean I confess I pick up the papers on this issue and I don't know what line to take. Too much back-story. Too many names with too many consonants. Tell me a bit more about Geoff.

PAULETTE. Oh he's solid, solid. He works incredibly hard, insanely.

ALAN. Where's he come from? Unionist?

PAULETTE. No. He taught, got into politics, campaigned tirelessly with all the NGOs despite what he says.

ALAN. How about his regional standing?

PAULETTE. Oh, they love him back in Coventry. Far more visible than most of us. I mean he doesn't look after himself, messed up his life for sure – wife's left him.

ALAN. Well you couldn't live with that. Obsessive.

PAULETTE. Yeah. It's all personal with him. I mean you flirt with stuff, causes, you get lobbied. But not Geoff; he finds out for himself. I have a lot of time for him.

GEOFF *has returned, hovering.*

ALAN. We hadn't finished our deliberations.

GEOFF. I intended to read you something.

PAULETTE. Is this strictly necessary?

He reaches into a file and pulls out a fax.

GEOFF. I received this at four in the morning. From an old friend of mine, Jean Kiyabe.

ALAN. Where does he come in?

GEOFF. He's a politican. Muntu, I suppose. Here: 'Geoffrey – ' (he calls me that) – It's from one of the camps on the Congo border. 'Hope you are well. Village arrived in total last week. Since then conditions very bad. Water is full of Typhus. No firewood as overcrowding has stripped land; food is powder and rationed; today three children died; cannot bury them so wrapped in plastic and taken in truck to be burned. The earth is pumice, can't break it; rain washed tarpaulins away. We have lost everything'.

PAULETTE. These are Muntu folk he's talking about?

GEOFF. Yes. The so-called perpetrators of Genocide. In flight for fear of their lives. No exact records of casualties but whole villages can't be accounted for. The Congo authorities calculate a refugee population of 50, 000 in three days and still rising. They're being picked off from the rear by Kanga armed with American small-arms. There are reports of mass graves. Here, he says, in conclusion: 'I pray the world will hear our prayers. We are like ghosts, and the world pays our tormentors. God bless you my friend'.

Pause.

Oh. I didn't get the drinks.

PAULETTE. Forget it.

ALAN *gets up.*

ALAN. I'm going to have to talk to a few people.

GEOFF. I accept that what I have to say is hard to swallow.

ALAN. Well as I say. Make a few calls. Geoff. Sometimes we need reminding what we're here for.

He shakes GEOFF*'s hand.*

OK. The Lithuanian delegation awaits. Be good children.

ALAN *goes.* GEOFF *embraces* PAULETTE.

PAULETTE. Don't muss me up.

GEOFF. Did I do well?

PAULETTE. You scored some brownie points.

GEOFF. Was I passionate?

PAULETTE. You were passionate but cogent.

GEOFF. I was fucking cogent.

PAULETTE. Your social skills are getting almost good.

GEOFF. I'm going to do alright at this game.

PAULETTE. Well don't push your luck.

GEOFF. And you. You're wonderful.

He kisses her lightly; she sighs.

PAULETTE. Just don't make me bloody regret it.

E *Coventry, several years earlier,* GEOFF *speaking to children.*

GEOFF. That's the Government school building. The Irundi Government under the Movement for Democratic Republicanism is working very hard to allow all children of your age and older in every part of this tiny country to go to school. (*Groans.*) Teaching them reading and writing. Teaching them the old songs and dances which were forbidden by the Europeans and church groups as super-stitious. And through this window you can just make out children of all ages even young adults, up to sixty of them, imagine that, in one class, many of them walking in the dawn from all the local settlements, barefoot perhaps, walking with smiles on their faces, such is their eagerness to learn.

Faint sound of children's noise.

I think we take all this for granted some times don't we? Not them, not here. The immaculately turned-out boys and girls. And imagine the dances, in the cool of evening, the dances.

Faint sound of clapping, music.

C *European Parliament (July) late.* PAULETTE *and* JEAN, *in the bar, a little drunk.*

JEAN. You are not taken Paulette? A woman like you?

PAULETTE. No one'd have me.

JEAN. Yet you are a beautiful woman, really.

PAULETTE. You're clearly tipsy.

JEAN. No, no. You have Irundi eyes. And mouth. A full mouth.

PAULETTE. I wouldn't know about that. I don't go further back than St Kitts.

JEAN. Oh no. You are an African woman. And your ancestors were taken for slaves.

PAULETTE. True enough. And look at me now, here, huh. God, I'm drunk too.

JEAN. In our country we were never taken as slaves to the whites.

PAULETTE. I didn't know that. That's worth knowing.

JEAN. Slaves only to ourselves. No, not ourselves, no. The Kanga.

PAULETTE. So Geoff said.

JEAN. If you humiliate a man he will strike back. That is a fact.

PAULETTE. Not always at the right target, perhaps. Besides it's more complex isn't it; I mean I don't know but as I understand it, what I've read, it's not as simple as this strict division you make, this division into – tribe versus tribe.

JEAN *laughs.*

JEAN. I don't understand you, the way you talk. You talk like Geoffrey.

PAULETTE. How do you mean? I talk…this is just the way I talk.

JEAN. No Paulette I do not understand you. Who are you? What is your *nation*?

PAULETTE. That's not a question I feel I need to answer.

JEAN. It is the first question we must answer. Tell me who you are.

PAULETTE. I'm, well, I'm British. Well with the usual hyphens.

JEAN *laughs, drinks.*

JEAN. And you and Geoffrey, yes, you and Geoffrey.

PAULETTE. There's nothing between me and Geoff. We are friends. Colleagues.

Pause.

JEAN. Excuse me I am drunk and tired and you say things.

PAULETTE. Well…of course.

JEAN. But I would like you to promise me something.

He leans over her.

PAULETTE. Don't. Handle me. Jean.

JEAN. Will you promise me something.

PAULETTE. Jean, this is really not appropriate –

JEAN (*loud*). Promise me.

PAULETTE. OK, OK, look just, calm down, OK.

JEAN. When the time comes you will protect me.

PAULETTE. I don't get you. Please take your hand off me.

JEAN. When the time comes.

A *The present; Bruxelles-Midi station café.* TIM *standing.*

GEOFF. Why don't we make a party? Stay up all night?

TIM. I've got to get to the hostel.

GEOFF. The hostel'll be closed. You stay with me.

TIM. I'll get a cab.

GEOFF. I have a bottle of Lagavullin back at the flat.

FLORENCE. OK, we are closed.

TIM. Strict curfew which I've already exceeded.

GEOFF. Constituency prezzie.

TIM. Besides we're getting the 8am to Schengen.

GEOFF (*to* FLORENCE). You could kip – where do you kip?

FLORENCE. 'Kip'? I don't –

GEOFF. Sleep over. At my flat. As we're all strangers here, someone's got to play host.

FLORENCE. I must go to my boss.

GEOFF. Fuck your boss.

TIM. Dad, what are you doing?

GEOFF. Fuck your boss and come and have some Lagavullin with my son and I.

TIM. You don't even know who she is.

GEOFF. What?

FLORENCE. Yes we close now.

TIM. She could be anyone. Surely you're advised against just…

GEOFF. What are you turning into Tim? Where's this fear come from?

TIM. You're pissed or something, dad.

GEOFF. Listen lad we have an absolute duty incumbent on us, the privileged – where you going?

TIM. I'll walk there and, maybe, maybe I'll see you.

GEOFF. I haven't bloody finished. You don't know your way around and your father who you never see or speak to your father is speaking to you. So you sit down.

TIM. I've heard the fucking speech dad.

GEOFF. Don't you swear at me, at your father –

TIM. I know about your fucking sense of duty to everybody who can spin a fucking yarn, everyone from somewhere that's about as far from us as you can get to.

GEOFF. I don't think you do, I don't think, I think you're turning into the sort of selfish little sod –

TIM. I'm starting my life now dad. OK? I'm trying things out.

GEOFF. Maybe you should start to ask a few bloody questions yeah? Stick your neck out a bit. What are you kids about, you know nothing, you live in a tiny world –

TIM. Shut-up. Shut up. You, you never change, you.

GEOFF. You know what Tim they won't take me down easy yeah I don't forget I'm not here for my convenience, this world is not a holiday, it's not a gap year, this world is asking questions of us, this world is sick of people like us, in places like this.

TIM. You are incapable of change.

TIM goes.

GEOFF. Don't tell me what I am. Don't you tell me what I am. Tim.

Silence. GEOFF *looks at* FLORENCE.

FLORENCE. You have lost your son.

C *Bar in European Parliament (July).* JEAN *has vomited on himself.*

JEAN. Dizzy. Excuse me.

GEOFF. OK mate?

PAULETTE. I'll get you something, some water, something.

JEAN. I am very well.

GEOFF. He's dizzy.

PAULETTE. Yes, water.

GEOFF. She'll get you some water.

PAULETTE. He's been in transit.

GEOFF. Eight hours from Uganda. Technicalities at Brussels.

PAULETTE. We ought to get you out of this building.

JEAN brushes himself down.

JEAN. This is my only suit.

GEOFF. I'll lend you one of mine.

PAULETTE. I'll get something to clean you up.

She goes.

JEAN. I have made a terrible mess. In this beautiful building.

GEOFF. Don't give it a thought. There's all sort of shit on these seats. All that midnight shagging between Dutch Greens and Danish Libertarians.

JEAN. What?

GEOFF. Nothing. Rubbish.

JEAN. I could never follow your words my friend.

GEOFF. I just want you to have a good time here. You've been through – terrible things.

Pause.

I saw footage, of the village.

JEAN. Please.

GEOFF. The church. The earth red beneath the church.

Pause.

It was all muddled up, what was said, the way they described it. But – heaps of bodies. I mean it was – what happened – can you – I mean where were you when –

JEAN. What do you think I was doing my friend?

Pause.

In one night the whole village was gone. In one night we fled. Like so many birds. Across the marshes, with our things in heavy bundles on our backs, our whole lives, all we could take, across the river –

GEOFF. There were reports of bodies in the water –

JEAN. Yes yes bodies bodies many dead many killed –

GEOFF. By whom?

JEAN. All killed all in fear in fear. It was war.

GEOFF. Of course, of course.

JEAN. And now who is dying –

GEOFF. Yes I say this –

JEAN. Our president assasinated our country invaded –

GEOFF. But the Kanga in Irundi they – died –

JEAN. Many people died Geoffrey, are dying. We all died.

Pause.

GEOFF. I've tried hard to maintain the line.

JEAN. You received my faxes?

GEOFF. Yes. It was good to have trustworthy sources.

JEAN. You have been a loyal friend to our people.

GEOFF. It's keeping it in focus.

JEAN. Without your kindness your interventions –

GEOFF. Don't say it. You don't need to say – it's good to *see* you.

GEOFF embraces JEAN.

JEAN. I would be a dead man. Without your kindness.

GEOFF. Ah, look at me. My suit too, now.

Wipes himself.

JEAN. Brothers, then, encore.

GEOFF. Yeah. Welcome to Europe brother.

Blackout.

TWO: AFRICA

A   *Irundi 1980. The porch of* JEAN*'s unfinished house.*

B   *Brussels, the present, March, later that night.* GEOFF*'s flat.*

A *Night.* ODETTE *cleaning the porch with a switch.* JEAN *and* GEOFF *enter,* GEOFF*, with a rucksack in shorts and t-shirt, shivering,* JEAN *with other bags.* ODETTE *takes bags.*

JEAN. Patrice, is a hell of a driver, huh?

GEOFF. He takes it at a lick.

JEAN. He once drove to the city in three hours.

GEOFF. I thought it was only 50 odd miles.

JEAN. Three hours is fast, man. When the rains come it can take a day, you get what are they – flats. Pffff!

GEOFF. Blow-outs. We had one.

JEAN. Patrice is fast. Unscrew the lock-nuts, off with the tyre, on with the new. Five minutes, finis. (*Claps.*)

GEOFF. No calling the A.A.

JEAN. I am sorry?

GEOFF. Sorry. I'm a bit out of it. I'd like to sleep.

JEAN. Of course.

GEOFF. The folk at London said I'd have a room.

JEAN. Yes. In here.

GEOFF. Oh.

JEAN. Patrice and I built this house. You will see there are two courses of brick, and plaster on the inside walls. The roof is not yet quite finished.

GEOFF. Yeah. I see.

JEAN. Our father's house was here before. Traditional style. Not sanitary. The new house is cooler. There will be room for my mother and perhaps Patrice's family and for now for you.

ODETTE *returns to cleaning the floor with a switch.*

As bourgmestre it is essential that I have a modern house where I may receive my guests.

GEOFF. What if it rains?

JEAN. Yes, it will rain in the night. The tarpaulin I think will hold. There is a bed prepared for you. There is water.

Picks up a jerry-can.

Tomorrow I wake you early, we eat, I take you to the children.

Pause. JEAN *sees* GEOFF *as if for the first time.*

JEAN. 'Geoffrey Fallon'. You are such a young fellow.

GEOFF. I'm 20.

JEAN. The Fathers said you would be a teacher. Our children need a teacher with wisdom.

GEOFF. I've been on a TEFL course.

JEAN. Your clothes are not warm!

GEOFF. I thought it would be hot.

JEAN. It is night! We are on a mountain here, my friend.

JEAN *laughs.*

GEOFF. Oh. OK.

JEAN. But it is good to have an Englishman.

GEOFF. It's excellent. You speaking such good English.

JEAN. Yes yes. I practise my English with you. Habitually it is Belgians, French, Canadians maybe – but French – but never English, and this saddens me, I say send us Englishmen, I speak this language, I am an Anglican.

GEOFF. You're Christian?

JEAN. Of course.

Awkward pause. GEOFF *uneasy under his rucksack.*

Ah, forgive me. I neglect you. Look at you, heavy burden that you have.

He takes it; GEOFF *keels.*

Please sit down, sit down my guest, my friend. A beer?

Shouts within.

Bières!

GEOFF. Ah that'd be ace.

ODETTE *appears with beers, opens them.*

JEAN. Beer, beer, so. (*Opens bottle, pours.*) Made with sorghum grown in this very soil.

GEOFF. Sore what?

JEAN. Sorghum. A grain. 'Primus' brew. You drink Primus in Europe?

GEOFF. I don't generally drink foreign stuff.

JEAN. Hey do not stand your bag is very heavy – what do you carry here huh – stones – you are a mule man, ah it weighs like stones, what do you carry?

GEOFF. Just books mainly. Textbooks.

JEAN *opens the bag and books fall out;* ODETTE *picks them up.*

It's OK.

JEAN. This is a library man.

GEOFF. Will they rot? I read that. That they rot.

JEAN. Books, books, books.

GEOFF. They're a bit dated. Handmedowns.

JEAN *looking through books.*

JEAN. This place is London, correct?

GEOFF. Yeah. Bright red buses beefeaters and shit.

JEAN. This? Where is this?

GEOFF. Oh, that's, hang on: 'Stratford-upon-Avon'.

JEAN. This lady is Queen Elizabeth the Second. But I think am right to say there is another lady who rules in your country.

GEOFF. Oh. Yeah, that'd be Thatcher.

JEAN. Who has the most power in your land? The Queen or Thatcher?

GEOFF. Good question. Technically speaking, Thatcher.

JEAN. Once we too were ruled by kings and queens. No longer. Why do your people accept this?

GEOFF. Because…well, it's complicated.

JEAN. OK. Useful books. In the lycée we read books by a Frenchman. Fontaine. You know this man's books?

GEOFF. I never paid much heed in French.

JEAN. I refused to read them. I fought the priests: 'Why must we read stories where animals talk? We are not children. We are a modern people'. But I talk about myself and you, you have come to us.

JEAN *takes another bottle of beer, forces the cap and pours it out on the ground, slowly.*

A drink. For the dead.

GEOFF. Oh right. Ancestor cult. Read about this too.

JEAN. They live here with us, the dead – in the walls, the earth, my father's bones are my soil and his father's bones his. There.

The bottle is empty.

GEOFF. Good to toast 'em.

JEAN *looks at him.*

JEAN. You think it is strange.

GEOFF. Oh no. Well, of course, in a way, sure. Better than ten minutes in the crematorium and an urn on your mantelpiece.

JEAN. Habits. Yes. Foolish perhaps.

GEOFF. Yeah but this is what it is, what we've lost. Like, folk knowledge, your intuitive your actual African –

JEAN. African?

GEOFF. As opposed to European. If you don't mind me saying – generalising.

They look at each other.

JEAN. You think I am a peasant?

GEOFF. No no, no I wasn't implying, and even if you were –

JEAN. My father worked the soil, OK. But I am not a peasant.

GEOFF. Obviously not.

JEAN. I am a civil servant.

GEOFF. Look look I know I mean – I mean I don't walk under ladders.

JEAN. Geoffrey I don't understand your words.

GEOFF. Geoff please. It's a crap enough name like that but –

JEAN. Geoffrey yes, a good name. You are sleepy, I will leave you, you need to sleep.

GEOFF. Before you go, hang on, I've got, got a present for you –

JEAN. Ah you are kind but I would not accept –

GEOFF. No, nothing much, just, I thought, well, mum's idea in fact –

He rummages in rucksack.

Shit – it's – wet – oh shit – it's – smashed. Lagavullin. Single malt. Prince Charles drinks it.

B GEOFF's *flat, Brussels, the present. The floor covered with papers;* FLORENCE *stands in doorway.*

GEOFF. What amounts to home.

She enters.

FLORENCE. Ah! It is wonderful. Yes, yes.

GEOFF. Stay here far more than I should, but then there's nothing to take me – back.

She's wandering around the space.

FLORENCE. Wonderful. But so cold.

GEOFF. Not bad for free, though. Well I get an allowance. Cold, yes, get some heat on. OK. (*Off.*) Where do you – kip – sleep?

FLORENCE. The patron has a room. Near the children. I wake with them, play with them.

GEOFF (*off*). Pays you for that does he?

FLORENCE. I eat with the children. They are very funny.

GEOFF (*off*). Indentured slavery. Jesus.

FLORENCE. No no he is kind. He will not go to the police.

GEOFF *re-enters, stoops to gather documents.*

GEOFF. You'd hardly know that this garbage holds the fate of nations. Here: Alan's paper, one of the guys I work with, infrastructural convergence in the Baltic states. He's hot on those Baltic states I tell you.

She bends too.

FLORENCE. I will organise this.

GEOFF. Doesn't matter, leave it.

FLORENCE. I place it in piles like so.

GEOFF. No. Leave it…I don't know your name.

FLORENCE. My name?

GEOFF. Yes.

FLORENCE. Florence.

GEOFF. Ah. A lovely name. I'm fond of the names in your country. Patrice, Melchior, Odette.

FLORENCE. They were given to us by priests.

Pause.

GEOFF. You know we could – I can speak Irundi, a little. Rustily.

FLORENCE. No. I do not want that. We will speak English.

GEOFF. It would bring back memories for me.

FLORENCE. For me also.

They look at each other. A stillness.

GEOFF. You should leave this boss of yours.

FLORENCE. He is my friend. He has need of me.

GEOFF. He'll find another. Employee.

FLORENCE. He shelters me.

GEOFF. Well, you could stop here. I come and go, all the time, Strasbourg, Coventry, never anywhere much, and this stays rented out, scandalous waste, you could stop here. Bags of room. They can't take it off me whatever happens.

FLORENCE: I cannot accept. I have no money.

GEOFF. There's no call for money. I, I want to, yes I want to.

FLORENCE. No I could not.

GEOFF. It's there, going begging.

FLORENCE. You do not know who I am.

GEOFF. I've got a pretty good notion.

Pause.

I'll get you a key cut.

FLORENCE. What about the authorities?

GEOFF. You in trouble?

FLORENCE. I do not have…the requisite…papers.

GEOFF. I have immunity here. This'll be a little bit of Europe that's entirely yours. Cops can't touch you.

FLORENCE. I will work for you then. And I will earn my rent –

GEOFF. No, no, no, I'm not getting into some sub-letting scam.

FLORENCE. I must repay you for your kindness.

GEOFF. Seriously no, just some practical, actual redistribution.

FLORENCE. I will serve you.

GEOFF. Don't be daft.

FLORENCE. Yes. Yes. I will cook, shop, clean, wash, tend. I will sort your papers into folders.

GEOFF. Well believe it or not I do have secretarial support.

FLORENCE. I will do all that you wish.

Pause.

GEOFF. You don't want to be too trusting of me.

FLORENCE. Yes I trust you. You trust me, so…

GEOFF. You know nothing about me.

FLORENCE. I know you have a son. You have a wife.

GEOFF. I had a wife. Separated. There, see.

FLORENCE. I will assist you. In your life and work. In your needs, the needs of a man.

She touches him; he steps away.

GEOFF. Well actually in my finest hours I profess to socialist feminist – principles which would sit pretty uneasily with bonded undeclared – servitude –

FLORENCE. I touched you.

GEOFF. Yes.

FLORENCE. Permit me to touch you.

This time he accepts.

I want you to touch me.

She begins to undress.

GEOFF. Stop it, don't, no you've got this wrong, I don't go in for – You will do nothing, you will accept it as your due, a little bit of the massive European cake, I mean how old are you, even?

FLORENCE. Too old. Too many lives I have lived all to be forgotten. My past until now is a nothing.

She strokes his face and hums an Irundi tune; he takes her hand, kisses her fingers.

GEOFF. Oh Christ. Jesus.

He kisses her, recoils.

You understand, you must understand – my intention – you are clear that I did not – lure you – here –

He kisses her again.

Do you really want this?

FLORENCE. I want what you want.

A *Early morning. Birdsong, cattle lowing, work-sounds.* GEOFF, *undressed on porch-step, taking photographs.*

GEOFF. My god. Amazing. Amazing.

ODETTE *enters with calabash of milk.*

Morning.

She nods, he conceals himself.

Came out early to get the light. 'De bonne heure.'

She offers the calabash; he accepts it.

Thanks. Thank you.

JEAN *enters; she moves into the house.*

JEAN. Good morning, good morning, good morning, it is
   already late.

GEOFF. Such an amazing light. Like being in a crystal. The
   peaks, they're so clear, they seem inches away.

JEAN. Good working day. It will rain by noon. The milk is
   fresh, drink it, drink. You slept deeply?

GEOFF. Oh, not bad. Very odd dreams, everything mixed up.

JEAN. My ancestors in your head: 'what is this European here
   now for? Another, another'.

   GEOFF *drinks the milk; spits it out.*

GEOFF. God it's sour, sorry, it's off, this.

JEAN. What – (*He drinks.*) – that milk is hot man, the teat raw
   in my hand. Drink.

GEOFF: Yeah. Of course. Be brave, Geoff. (*He drinks.*) OK.
   Tasty.

JEAN. Finish it. It is all yours.

GEOFF. Too generous.

JEAN. You will need the strength. All of it.

   GEOFF *drinks more.*

   Today we clear trees from the slopes, find new soil, burn
   back the bush, there, on the slope.

GEOFF. Can you work land like that? Must be a one-in- ten
   incline.

JEAN. No land goes unturned. Many mouths and little soil.
   The directives say grow in bulk, root out peasant
   techniques; this is what I read. I study Agronomy.

GEOFF. Won't you get leaching? With the rains?

JEAN. No, no. The problem is land division.

   JEAN *draws patterns in the dust.*

In the old ways each peasant had his own plot, so, so. A little piece for cassava, for sorghum maybe, a little for maize, for banana. Yeah? The Europeans kept the plains, gave the best pasture for Kanga cattle. The Muntu lived on the bad land. And when a farmer died the sons would divide the land so and so and so and the land grew as small and small as this.

He wipes out the traces.

Our modern way is to unify the land, big community plots, more pesticide, high-yields, yeah, and then export export, get currency in, more investment and so the country grows and grows and the people grow fatter. But the soil is so poor, and there are too many people on too little soil. And we will grow pyrethrum, fast-growth, for export; and coffee and sorghum for beer –

GEOFF. Should export your beer, certainly.

JEAN. Yes beer.

GEOFF. Leaves you with a wicked head.

JEAN. Beer, tea, pyrethrum. All for export. But it is now time to work, not for words; school starts at seven.

GEOFF. I'll get dressed. Give me a couple of minutes.

JEAN. You have secrets from me?

GEOFF. No just the usual regular parts.

JEAN. You won't blind me, you with your white skin, yes, you are made of milk man.

GEOFF *starts scrabbling into clothes.*

GEOFF. Always been on the pale side.

JEAN. Look at you, long and skinny like a Kanga.

GEOFF. OK. Nothing to hide amongst fellow men.

JEAN. A good height is a lucky thing. I am lucky. But you have no flesh on you.

GEOFF. Just as God made me, yeah.

JEAN. OK. When Kanga are born you know they are like Muntu, short and heavy, but the mothers pull their soft bones and skin and pull and pull their arms, their legs right out – so, so, like gum.

GEOFF. Sounds a bit implausible.

JEAN. No, Geoffrey, not at all. Take the women. The women are proven to be different by the Government. The church has condemned these Kanga women.

GEOFF. Churches tend to do that.

JEAN. Condemned for their folk practices.

GEOFF. You don't swallow that stuff!

JEAN. I know what I know. The young girls who take twigs of birch down down to their women's lips, here, yes, turning and stretching and pulling, like this. You understand? For their pleasure and the wicked pleasure of their husbands.

He simulates a woman masturbating. GEOFF *laughs nervously.*

GEOFF. You're taking the mickey.

JEAN. I'm very serious about this.

A tinny carillon in the distance.

You must dress faster. Class will begin.

GEOFF. 'S early. My brain's not up 'fore nine.

JEAN. I'll walk there, you and I walk together.

GEOFF. Should I wear my suit?

He pulls a crumpled suit from the rucksack.

Stinks of whisky.

JEAN. Of course, you are the teacher.

GEOFF. Yes. I suppose I am.

GEOFF dresses.

JEAN. They must respect you. The boys walk for many miles at first sun, to the new school.

GEOFF. It's a grey old thing.

JEAN. Yes, I insisted, walls of cool concrete, new windows.

GEOFF. Could do with a roof as well.

JEAN. They come, through the bush, hungry for new words, your words.

GEOFF*'s dressed in the crumpled suit.*

GEOFF. Hope I'm worth the walk.

JEAN. Oh yes yes, they learn you teach we learn and I plant pyrethrum and the world and life gets better every day.

B *Darkness;* FLORENCE *and* GEOFF *undressing each other.*

GEOFF. I can hardly see you. Just your teeth.

FLORENCE. My teeth. There. Like a crocodile.

Laughs.

GEOFF. Look orange. In the light.

FLORENCE. I don't need to see you. I can feel you. Your weight.

GEOFF. Great fat heap.

FLORENCE (*laughs*). Yeah, good and fat.

GEOFF. Oh ta. Don't be kind.

FLORENCE. And hairy very very hairy.

They laugh; they kiss.

Do we make love now? I think you would like to.

GEOFF. That's clear enough. Jesus. And that's rare.

FLORENCE. Just for me then. Your cock is ready for me, huh?

She lies back, masturbates a bit.

Mmm now I am ready.

He lies on her, kisses her.

I'll help you. There.

GEOFF. No hang on. Wait.

FLORENCE. Wait? No, now.

GEOFF. No. God.

FLORENCE. Please…

GEOFF. Much as I'd – God – I don't have – I'm a twat –

FLORENCE. What are you saying?

GEOFF. I don't have any protection.

FLORENCE. Protection?

GEOFF. No rubbers, no.

Pause. FLORENCE *sits up.*

FLORENCE. You think I'm sick. Inside.

GEOFF. No, no. Well, either of us could be.

FLORENCE. I might be a whore, sure. I can be a whore for you.

GEOFF. You don't know, I wouldn't know what I've picked up along the way.

FLORENCE. Ah so you have slept with many.

GEOFF. Not really no.

She kisses him and tastes his spit.

FLORENCE. There. It's OK. Use my hands.

She starts masturbating him.

I make the sea in your balls flow, hey.

GEOFF. No. That's not…on the right terms.

She pulls away.

FLORENCE. What is it that you want?

GEOFF. I could pop out and get – some. From the tabac, there's a –

FLORENCE. I say I am not sick!

She moves away.

GEOFF. I'm sure. Of course.

He caresses her.

GEOFF. There'll be time. There's plenty of time for all of this.

FLORENCE. There is only now.

She embraces him hard.

GEOFF. All these years I've never – made love – to an African.

FLORENCE. I am not Africa monsieur.

GEOFF. No, of course not. But. You can never truly understand another people, a world without giving up your most private desires and touching and going – over. Totally. Touching. Knowing. I think.

FLORENCE. A woman is not a nation.

GEOFF. Ah. You're like velvet. Peach.

FLORENCE. You're like silk. Paper. (*She feels his torso.*) Is this Europe, then? Your stomach. Huh?

GEOFF. Yeah yeah – slack and flabby and scarred.

FLORENCE. You have scars, yes. What is this one? (*On his forehead.*)

GEOFF. Oh stood up too soon in a cave, when I was little.

FLORENCE. And on your hand?

GEOFF. Garden accident.

She holds his arm up.

FLORENCE. And here?

GEOFF. That. That's a souvenir. From your homeland.

Pause.

FLORENCE. I have these souvenirs too.

GEOFF. Yes on your back yes. Deep. Do you want to tell me – ?

FLORENCE. No. No. Only this night.

A *Late afternoon.* ODETTE *preparing food singing.* GEOFF *enters, hot. They look at each other.*

GEOFF. Right. Is Jean – Jean?

She shakes her head.

ODETTE. Dehors.

GEOFF. Sorry?

She gestures.

GEOFF. Oh. OK. D'accord.

Pause.

Can I – ?

He points at the cooking.

ODETTE. Ce n'est pas prête.

GEOFF. No. I mean – can – I – aider?

ODETTE. Comment?

She giggles, he too. He approaches as if to help, she stops him.

ODETTE. Non non – ce n'est pas juste.

GEOFF *gets out pocket dictionary.*

GEOFF. C'est bon ici – mais très, très – chaud. Hot.

She shrugs.

ODETTE. Peut-être mais la natation est possible, dans le lac –

GEOFF. Pardon, pardon – err – lentement –

ODETTE. Natation. Nager. Possible.

He rummages in dictionary. She mimes swimming.

GEOFF. Ah yes, yes, swimming, yes.

ODETTE. Dans le lac.

GEOFF. The lake. Do you – nager?

ODETTE. Oui, oui quelquefois, de bonne heure, oui.

Silence. She shrugs, then sings tune again.

ODETTE. Vous avez soif?

GEOFF. Oh – sorry – yeah – soif – yeah, a bit, yeah.

ODETTE. Vous aimez le Fanta?

GEOFF. Fanta. What – like Lilt – 'the totally tropical taste'? Yeah.

ODETTE. Non, non Fanta ici.

She gives him a bottle of standard soft drink.

GEOFF. Oh ta. Cheers. (*He drinks.*) Bit tepid. Want some?

ODETTE. Moi?

GEOFF. Want some?

ODETTE. Non c'est pour toi. Le patron.

GEOFF. Have some.

She cautiously takes it and drink.

ODETTE. Ah, c'est – délicieux.

GEOFF. 'Sonly a bit of pop.

ODETTE. Merci, merci beaucoup.

GEOFF. Well, it's just –

Her head is bent. Embarassed silence.

Qu'est-que c'est? Pour manger?

ODETTE. Chèvre?

GEOFF. Shevre? What's that – chicken?

Looks in dictionary.

Can't see 'shevre'.

She makes horns; laughs; he laughs.

Oh, it's got horns. What? A cow? Vache?

She mimes a beard.

GEOFF. Goat. Right. 'Chèvre'. Of course.

ODETTE. Ah oui oui, le chèvre, oui.

ODETTE *prepares the food on an old stove; he watches.*

GEOFF. Funny day. Good day. I think. Some of the lads, some of them older than me, still in school poor bastards taught by me. Just conversation stuff and that.

He prepares a rolly.

GEOFF. Want one of these?

ODETTE. D'accord.

He rolls her one.

So I did this exercise, just to get 'em talking like, err – and the thing is with 'em, when they laugh, you feel what was that about? Are we laughin' about – y'know. I'll be honest, forty big black lads, brick shithouses all, pretty intimidating.

Lights her cigarette; she smokes.

So this exercise, you're thinking what do we talk about – yeah tell me what is your nation, what it means – to you – Kanga, Muntu, whatever. I mean, I assume the Kanga kids come there too. I mean you're –? Vous êtes…?

ODETTE. Moi?

GEOFF. Vous êtes Kanga? Oui?

She stops work and looks at him.

ODETTE. Ah oui. Oui monsieur. Kanga. Lineage des rois anciens de l'ancien royaume Irundi.

GEOFF. I didn't really get any of that.

ODETTE. Kanga. Lineage des rois. Ce n'importe.

She returns to work.

GEOFF. So I said, OK, in your own words, your personal
    words, 'What is my Nation?'. Mood changed, dead hush,
    there and then, like you'd trespassed onto something and the
    biggest lad, Laurent, six foot odd, comes up, others part for
    him, dead proud, comes up to where I was stood, forty eyes
    on us, me, first lesson, whatever and he says 'Muntu once
    low and now tall; Muntu once slave, now king; Muntu clear
    bush away, burn out the – *'inyazi'* – *'inyazi'?*

ODETTE. *Inyenzi.*

    She nods; she's very still.

GEOFF. Yeah. That's it. Yeah. Qu'est que c'est?

    She shrugs. He looks fully at her.

    Restez-là.

ODETTE. Pourquoi?

    He takes his camera out.

GEOFF. L'image. Tres belle, comme ça.

ODETTE. Non. Ce n'est pas juste.

GEOFF. Just…quickly. Travailler. Comme avant…travailler.

    She works; he takes a picture. JEAN *enters with a machete
    (panga).*

JEAN. Qu'est que tu fais ici – huh?

GEOFF. We were just chatting. I was just – chatting.

JEAN. She does not speak your language.

GEOFF. No. We weren't making too much sense.

JEAN. She has many tasks to do. You take pictures of her?

    ODETTE *tries to move inside unnoticed;* JEAN *takes*
    GEOFF*'s camera.*

GEOFF. To show people back home. How you live here.

JEAN. OK, Geoffrey. You like this girl? I take a picture for
    you? You two yeah?

GEOFF. No, no – well…

JEAN. She's tall, like you. Maybe she likes you.

GEOFF. You've got this wrong.

JEAN. That's OK man. Take pictures. Restez-ici. Together. You can hold her.

GEOFF. That's not necessary.

JEAN. Souris pour le gentilhomme.

ODETTE *and* GEOFF *in stilted poses.*

Hold her man. It's good. Good shot.

GEOFF. No you've got the wrong end of the stick.

GEOFF *snatches the camera;* ODETTE *goes.*

JEAN. It's OK. She is no one's. She is not taken.

GEOFF. It was just for the image, the image of – I don't know. An African woman. As if I wasn't there. Entirely herself.

JEAN. But you are here Geoffrey. You look. You want to look. Good. A woman is to be looked at.

Pause.

GEOFF. You know what we'd call you back home. Sexist.

B GEOFF *and* FLORENCE *lie on the floor, sharing a cigarette.*

GEOFF. Tell me things.

FLORENCE. Why do you ask me questions?

GEOFF. Every word you say restores me. Every fact about how you lived. Not the violence. I know about that. That we know about. We rehearse this violence over and over, to frighten ourselves, to remind ourselves how these cold European lives are all there is, all there can be, however dead, however bloody dry, are all that can be hoped for. I think your being happy would scare us. You wouldn't need us and it would scare us. I think.

He sits up.

Tell me about your life. Everyday things. Your family?

FLORENCE. Father was a scientist. Worked for *Electrogaz*. Big Government company. Mother was a school err 'inspecteur'?

GEOFF. Same word, yeah. Tell me about your mother.

FLORENCE. She returned the old ways to the children. The dances, the songs.

GEOFF. Stuff the Belgians killed off.

FLORENCE. She travelled from village to village.

GEOFF. You went with her?

FLORENCE. Yes. A baby, on her back, close to her warmth, hearing her voice, boom boom and laughing, boom boom.

They laugh. Silence.

GEOFF. Don't stop. It makes me so happy, I dunno, just hearing you talk, God it's like – music.

Kisses her.

FLORENCE. I will cry if I keep talking.

GEOFF. Maybe that's a good thing.

Silence.

FLORENCE. Villages, all different, all the same. In the North, the Lake country, the forest lands, the plains. She would say, 'look the people have grown ashamed, we have grown ashamed of ourselves, our ancestors, now we must sing their songs again, grow strong again'.

GEOFF. I remember so much music, yes.

He hums a tune; she smiles, joins him.

FLORENCE. I know this tune.

GEOFF. It's hard, the scale's hard, different scale.

FLORENCE. Like this.

She sings.

She would say, the White Fathers teach us their songs and we sang them always wrong, always 'out of tune'. No, no she told us, children, people, your music is a different music a different scale, but still music, be proud of your music!

GEOFF. Yes.

FLORENCE. And she taught again the dances that were soon to be lost, learned dances from the old, the dying ones. See children; the dance of sowing, the dance of harvest – see –

She creates a rhythm of sowing.

Sowing the sorghum seed, knees bent and you sow and sow and sow and sow. You do this dance with me?

GEOFF. No no I don't dance. I can't – dance.

FLORENCE. Everyone dances, follow me – it is easy –

GEOFF. No. No I can't.

FLORENCE. Yes, yes, it is a child's dance, very simple, so.

She takes him, shows him her dance.

I see her going into the schools and children run to her laughing and she sits under a tree swatting away flies and plays a drum, talking talking – 'alors mes enfants'. Her bright print dress.

GEOFF. Which tradition? I mean the dances – were they – Muntu no, they must have been Kanga. Kanga?

Silence.

FLORENCE. The Europeans ask always which tribe and 'who are you, this or that'? Irundi has one language, one faith, one culture.

GEOFF. Even now?

Pause.

Sorry. Sorry. Fuck. Sorry.

FLORENCE. When you speak you become known.

GEOFF. I just want to know about you.

FLORENCE. I have spoken too many things.

GEOFF. I want to know you. Who you are? You studied? Florence? You were a student and then you came here? Yes?

FLORENCE. I studied. At University. I was there when – before.

GEOFF. And what did you study?

FLORENCE. Theology. God's language.

GEOFF. Ah.

FLORENCE. Yes. Is it not amazing that this was my life? Reading. Who was saved. Who could be saved. God's time. Our stories and Jesus' stories. The meaning of the cross. This, I wrote about. The Cross, Mission, salt of the earth, light to the world, salt and light. It makes me happy to think of my work.

She's crying.

GEOFF. I'm taking advantage of you. Yeah.

He starts to dress.

Look I'll sleep – in the – through there. You have this –

She's crying still.

I'm sorry. Here. I'm sorry.

He embraces her.

FLORENCE. I want to live.

GEOFF. You – will – we'll –

FLORENCE. What I have done I have done.

GEOFF. Of course. Of course.

A *Later, the meal finished, bottles empty.* ODETTE *clears away.*

GEOFF. Very nice. Bien.

JEAN. Good that you liked it. It was killed for you. Tomorrow it's manioc.

GEOFF. Let me help.

JEAN. No you sit there. You have worked hard today. The boys told me of your lesson. A good day. Odette, suffit.

She goes.

GEOFF. I do think – the way you – treat – her – I just – think – I dunno.

JEAN. You think, you don't know – what?

GEOFF. It seems – very – hard.

Silence. JEAN *cleans and oils his panga.*

It's none of my business.

JEAN. It's my business, right. Right.

GEOFF. Where I come from –

JEAN. What?

GEOFF. England. Europe. We consider –

JEAN. Europe. Yes. Progress.

GEOFF. I'm talking about rights.

JEAN. Rights? Progress.

GEOFF. Progress maybe, what's beneficial to – the majority, yes.

JEAN. Good, good, my words, my thoughts: help the majority.

GEOFF. Not excluding minorities though. In terms of rights.

JEAN. This nation is a republic of God for the majority.

GEOFF. Sure, I respect that.

JEAN. Egalite.

GEOFF. Yes. Same for all.

JEAN. Yes. For the loyal.

Pause.

Father was beaten every day. With a chicotte. Not by
Europeans. Beaten before his children. Watching their
cattle. Less than a man. Taking out their shit at night.
Odette's people. Not for money, my friend. In this village.
Beaten, like a beast. I saw it, as a young young boy. My
father kicked. How you treat a dog. A young boy seeing
his father kicked. Not by the whites! For the whites maybe
but by their lackeys. And even the priests said this is wrong.
All men are equal before their God. Correct?

GEOFF. Absolutely right.

JEAN. And we drove them out! With our hands. Not with guns
and bombs. First the Europeans and then their parasites.
Drove them out!

GEOFF. The revolution.

JEAN. Built a republic of god for the majority people.

GEOFF. Yes, yes. I see. I mean you stumble in, you aren't told
things. I honestly know so little.

JEAN. There will be time to learn.

JEAN *holds out the panga.*

GEOFF. What?

JEAN. Cut me.

GEOFF. What?

JEAN. It's good to do so. Here, see Patrice has a mark on me.
Now you. Yes, come. The blade is clean.

GEOFF. I can't do that.

JEAN. There's no pain. See.

JEAN *makes an incision on his arm.*

Look. The blade is fine. So, my blood. Come here.

GEOFF *approaches;* JEAN *takes his arm.*

Permit me.

GEOFF. What?

JEAN. I wish to be your friend. Do you wish to be mine? You sleep in my house. You teach my family. I consider you my brother. So, be my brother. Come.

GEOFF. You say it doesn't hurt.

JEAN. A light light touch. And then we are known to each other. As men.

Pause.

GEOFF. OK, I've given blood, I'm not that fucking squeamish, OK.

His arm out; JEAN *cuts;* GEOFF *winces;* JEAN *spits on hand and rubs blood together.*

JEAN. Trust me. Trust our ways.

GEOFF. Yes. I mean I'm a stranger here.

Pause.

JEAN. Let's drink.

GEOFF. OK. Cheers. To Jean.

JEAN. To Geoffrey. To Europe.

GEOFF. Fuck Europe.

JEAN. 'Fuck Europe'?

GEOFF. To you. To your people.

JEAN. To my people. OK.

GEOFF. To Irundi. Your country.

They drink; JEAN *laughs.*

JEAN. My country, yeah.

GEOFF. That's strong. Jesus.

JEAN. My country! Today I call the work party –

GEOFF. I saw you; you took half my class.

JEAN. Oh yeah, all the guys, off any detail, all the strong guys.

GEOFF. Freaked me out, young boys wielding these things.

He picks up the machete, plays with it.

JEAN. Brothers, equal and ready to work. Bush clearance.

GEOFF. No half-measures either, no work to rule. Out the door.

JEAN. No question. I whistle, they come.

GEOFF. Like it was China, or your Soviets, in the early days.

JEAN. Working, hacking, clearing.

GEOFF. I mean in that heat too, I was sweating cobs.

JEAN. All the land must work, we live in each other's shoes, and every day new mouths to feed –

GEOFF. Saw the smoke on the slopes, heard the work songs.

JEAN. We must push forward must be self-sufficient, and then strong, strong.

GEOFF. Break the whole cash-crop syndrome, right.

JEAN. At the top comes this old fella, Kanga, yes, all bones, bony shit cow drops its shit at our feet, I say, shift old man, this land is not for you, go; no answer; old fella look here, this is an official document from your Government, your capital city, dispossession order, so move your bony ass NOW; OK?

GEOFF *giggles.*

GEOFF. Silly obstinate git.

JEAN. Yes! Yes.

Drinks, belches, JEAN *drinks.*

JEAN. He says, to me, and the guys he says: 'Oohhh, ohhh, I never knew about this, about this place' 'Your capital city, old man, yes?' 'No no never have I heard of this place.' 'I have here a document from your Government, the ruling

party of the Movement for Democratic Republicanism'
'Ohh I never hear of this Government, is this from the
White Men, or the King?' Now I am angry: 'Old man
the kings are gone and dead and we are in a modern
DEMOCRACY and this is a document from your leader
and he say you cannot keep your cows here cos this is now
Government land and we will grow a new crop –
pyrethrum' and he say 'Ohh but my cow is here and my
father's cow and once I was a king of this place' – this old
piece of shit, face like old leather, cow just ribs and flies,
the guys sweating behind me, all hot and ready with the
pangas and – *Imana!*

He drinks his beer. Silence.

GEOFF. Surprised you didn't whop him one.

JEAN. No, no, I am in the civil service and we live in a
democratic republic and I say 'Old man we pay you money
for your cow and you live happy and old and drink *Primus*
beer until you die'.

GEOFF. Generous terms.

JEAN. He says:'This cattle is my kingdom.'

They drink.

GEOFF. He'll die soon enough. I expect.

JEAN. I hope so.

They laugh.

GEOFF. 'This cattle is my kingdom.'

GEOFF *plays with the panga;* ODETTE *watches.*

Have at ya!

JEAN. Careful man, careful. It is a weapon also.

GEOFF. Sure, sure. 'Panga.' (*Giggles.*)

JEAN. Yes. Hold it like this. Like so. And sweep sweep sweep.

GEOFF. Sweep sweep sweep.

JEAN. There Geoffrey. You are learning fast.

B GEOFF *stands over* FLORENCE *who moans to herself in her sleep, stirring, crying, laughing, suddenly shrieking. She sits up.* GEOFF *hovers by her.*

GEOFF. Florence? Florence. Wake – wake up – you're – dreaming.

She scrambles around; he tries to hold her still.

GEOFF. It's over, it's over – hey – it's over – dreams, dreams – it's over – still, still.

She sobs and sobs; comes round – sees him.

FLORENCE. Qui êtes vous? Qu'est que c'est ici – où suis – ? Où? Where where –?

GEOFF. It's OK. You're safe.

FLORENCE. Where am I?

GEOFF. You're with me. In safe hands. In a safe place. You're quite quite safe.

Blackout.

Interval.

THREE: EUROPE

A *The present.* ALAN *Carswell's office in the European Parliament building, the previous night.*

B *The present.* GEOFF's *flat, the following morning.*

A GEOFF *and* PAULETTE *sit in silence; two reports and glasses of water on table before them.*

GEOFF. I'm seeing Tim later. First time in a while. He's travelling.

PAULETTE. Hope the snow doesn't hold him up.

Pause.

GEOFF. I'd prefer not to be late.

PAULETTE. Alan won't have long.

Pause.

GEOFF. You've read this of course.

PAULETTE. I don't think we should discuss this until he gets here.

GEOFF. Right. Protocol.

PAULETTE. Yes.

Pause.

GEOFF. I should say I don't feel you need to take any responsibility for me or for what occurred –

PAULETTE. It's too late for that.

GEOFF. Not that I think that there's any foundation for the accusations levelled in here –

PAULETTE. The testimony of hundreds of witnesses tirelessly taken by independent international bodies.

GEOFF. Yeah well that's how it's dressed up.

PAULETTE. Oh Geoff.

Pause.

GEOFF. But if you feel compromised, I'd understand –

PAULETTE. Please.

GEOFF *sighs, gets up.*

Isn't it time you bought yourself a better suit?

GEOFF. It serves its purpose.

PAULETTE. I worry about you.

GEOFF. Glad someone does, love.

PAULETTE. I think you're incapable of simple human happiness.

Pause.

Can I make a suggestion? About this meeting?

GEOFF. Lost cause.

PAULETTE. Alan'll play it amiable.

GEOFF. Yeah, smooth operator Alan.

PAULETTE. Well it's more than style actually. He went a long way with you.

GEOFF. Good of him.

PAULETTE. Geoff listen up. Much of what this is about is saving face. Yeah?

GEOFF. It's too late for retractions even if I was up for it. Too many open letters to *The Guardian* and memos on file and Alan's seen the way the wind's blowing, end of this year I'll be in a black hole at the bottom of the candidate list –

PAULETTE. Geoff there's something a bit deeper at stake here.

GEOFF. No no it's all headline management.

PAULETTE. For God's sake do yourself some favours, you don't need to get messed up in this, this mess, you did what you did in good faith, but this –

GEOFF. That, whatever that is, is in dispute actually –

PAULETTE. You dispute the body-count?

GEOFF. Look I never disputed that I – ?

PAULETTE. Don't you feel just a little bit soiled, a little bit used – I know I do. This man touched me. Did I tell you that?

GEOFF. He misread the signs.

PAULETTE. He came on to me. I mean that's not the point.

GEOFF. He was drunk. He was far from home.

PAULETTE. That's not what I'm saying.

GEOFF. He's a fucking human being.

PAULETTE. God!

Pause.

I'm starting to wonder where your limit is Geoff.

B GEOFF's *flat, early morning;* GEOFF, *dressed, looks at* FLORENCE *stirring.*

FLORENCE. Qu'est que c'est…?

GEOFF. You had a bad night.

He kisses her; she shivers.

But it's good you slept. You slept very deeply.

FLORENCE. Yes I slept well.

Pause.

GEOFF. Want some coffee? There's no milk.

FLORENCE. I'll make it, I can get milk.

GEOFF. I don't take it so's not a problem for you –

FLORENCE. No, no, what time is it?

GEOFF. Eightish.

FLORENCE. I should go and see my patron – I am – late –

GEOFF. We agreed you wouldn't.

FLORENCE. He will report me. He said this.

GEOFF. He's probably already got some replacement. Look I feel like having the works for breakfast, are you hungry –

FLORENCE. I am fine.

GEOFF. Patisseries, jus d'orange, waffles what do you fancy?

FLORENCE. I will buy these necessaries for you.

GEOFF. No you won't you'll have a shower and you'll – relax.

She gets up and hides her nakedness.

You're shy of me today.

FLORENCE. Pardon.

She lets the sheet slip.

GEOFF. No, no that wasn't a request – I hope you didn't feel I forced anything last night.

FLORENCE. No no I am grateful to you.

She nods, tries a smile.

GEOFF. Last night, when you were slept, you were, do you remember, you…

FLORENCE. I said things?

GEOFF. Yes, yes, it's ok, it's –

FLORENCE. What did I say?

GEOFF. I couldn't make it out.

FLORENCE. Just dreams, dreaming, only.

GEOFF. I know what happened in your country, I can well understand how hard, how difficult – talking – must be.

Pause.

What I'm trying to say is I know no one escaped unscathed,
and I feel, well it's hard to say this, this'll sound arrogant,
I feel for my own part, and I don't want to get into details,
I feel responsible, yes, responsible, to a degree, for what
happened, or what might have happened to you, Odette and
if you can tell me – tell me –

FLORENCE. My name is not Odette.

GEOFF. Ah. No. Of course not. Stupid. Florence.

A ALAN *with a tray of coffees.*

ALAN. There. Espresso, machiatto, cappuccino.

GEOFF. Cheers.

PAULETTE. Thank you.

They drink.

ALAN. Apologies for the late hour. I hope to move fast for the
press's purposes. Paulette, you take minutes.

GEOFF. I thought this was off the record.

ALAN. Everything must be minuted from now on.

PAULETTE. It's for your good too.

GEOFF. I don't have a problem with it.

ALAN. Good. Let's start then. The bottom line is I need to go
to press on this before the Dailies, which gives us a couple
of hours, as I've got a few folk standing by on the
Nationals. Paulette you circulate all relevant Party leaders,
the EU press, Commission; essentially the outcomes should
be twofold, a good and robust press release and a signed
round robin denunciation.

GEOFF. Hang on –

ALAN. Yes?

GEOFF. You're making a few assumptions here Alan.

ALAN. Yes, yes I have; you think I shouldn't –

GEOFF. I suspect you're taking things at face value.

ALAN. What?

Pause.

PAULETTE. Geoff has some responses to the dossier.

ALAN. I should bloody hope so.

GEOFF *stands.*

GEOFF. Well if you –

ALAN. You sit down.

GEOFF *sits.*

GEOFF. What is this, a kangaroo court? Did you minute that Paulette? What's at stake here, the truth or our backs?

ALAN. Ah. You're quite right Geoff, your objections, such as they are must be heard. But forgive me if I seek to clarify a few things that've been brought to my attention in the last few hours.

He gets the report out.

Where are we? Yes, it's a detail really but a critical one. Can we turn to Appendix 3.

They read.

ALAN. Am I reading this rightly Geoff?

GEOFF. It's pretty clear.

ALAN. So, OK, so after the visit of Monsieur Kiyabe to the European Parliament which we hosted and funded at your request and after this visit, this Kiyabe chap went to ground –

GEOFF. He requested Asylum.

PAULETTE. Leave to remain.

GEOFF. Which was granted.

ALAN. After a submission by you. To the Home Office. Correct?

GEOFF. I wrote on his behalf.

ALAN. Ending up in your patch. Bedworth.

GEOFF. Initially. He then went on to be reunited with his brother Patrice in Canada.

ALAN. I don't actually remember discussing that.

GEOFF. Well the response to his visit was so positive that I felt I had the backing of the party –

ALAN. You felt this but you didn't get it cleared.

GEOFF. I talked with Paulette –

PAULETTE. Yes that's right, we discussed settling him in the community –

ALAN. Don't minute that.

PAULETTE. I have played my part.

ALAN. This is not the issue is it Geoff?

GEOFF. No.

Pause.

ALAN. Yeah here's the bit I liked: 'M. Kiyabe has expressed his gratitude for the kind offices of MEP Geoff Fallon in his overtures to the British Government, and the warmth of the people of Bedworth'. This was before he scarpered.

GEOFF. The CLP set up a Benefit fund. We had jumble sales, fêtes, people threw sponges at me, kids sang Irundi songs. It was a deeply moving display of solidarity.

ALAN. And did you tell them where the money was headed?

GEOFF. What do you think? My team are renowned for fund-raising for causes embarrassing to party folk –

ALAN. And subbing a quiet retirement for a mass murderer fitted that profile very nicely.

GEOFF. That is a load of emotive bollocks.

PAULETTE. Geoff take that back.

ALAN. No it's ok, it is pretty emotive stuff really. Let's leave that, let's have a look at the report shall we.

GEOFF. Can I just get down some objections first?

Pause.

ALAN. I'd be very interested to hear your objections.

GEOFF. Yeah I've been taking notes on it, although frankly I'd need time and I didn't get all the appendices I don't think.

PAULETTE. You got the crucial sections.

GEOFF. Well, OK, but if we note that and just turn to page 5, which describes the commune where Jean was Bourgmestre, (not mayor incidentally, a different function, but that's not material), anyway, the first phrase here I objected to was 'a loosely assembled settlement of mixed racial composition'; just to question the term race here as in itself a racist and ethnographic inaccuracy; that's one –

ALAN. How many do you have? Objections.

GEOFF. Oh. Fifty odd.

ALAN. Right. All semantic quibbles?

GEOFF. They add up to a devastating portrait of shoddy research, conceptual muddle and slander.

ALAN. I see. So we better hear them. But quickly.

GEOFF. Page 7 (I'm leaving minor points out): 'Kiyabe was a member of extreme right organisation the CDR, Coalition to Defend the Republic'; the term 'extreme right' is in no way applicable to a broadly-based, class-based socialist organisation dedicated to the speedy realisation of Developmental goals and rooting out corruption. Yeah also on page 7 'Kiyabe was notorious for his separatist educational policy' – it goes on to use the highly specious term 'apartheid', and I know for a fact that Jean, I mean Kiyabe, made numerous overtures to Kanga community leaders rebuffed on each occasion, in fact I have here his paper on that, here, in, hang on –

He rummages in his brief-case, drops his papers; they stare at him; he looks up.

PAULETTE. Geoff, please.

GEOFF. Hang on, sorry, it's in here, sorry.

PAULETTE. Geoff for God's sake.

GEOFF. What?

ALAN *stands. A silence.*

What you don't seem to understand is this deposition that you have swallowed whole is littered with factual error –

ALAN. You said this –

GEOFF. Misattributions, bogus ethnic categorisation –

ALAN. Yes yes, got the point, yes –

GEOFF. Lurid reportage without context –

ALAN. Jesus wept.

Pause.

PAULETTE. What I want to say is, I felt so – sick – reading this, I – couldn't – get through it – I.

ALAN. It is unspeakable, truly.

Pause.

GEOFF. Yes. And to that extent it should be exposed as the inflammatory –

PAULETTE. I want to read you something. I want you to hear what I read and I want to see your face as I read it.

ALAN. I think we might be wasting our time.

PAULETTE. No no Geoff has acted from impeccable motives I just think he he –

GEOFF. Don't you dare PATRONISE me; *my* motives! My motives are neither here nor there.

ALAN. Now you just calm right down Geoff.

Pause.

PAULETTE. You perhaps haven't seen the wood for the trees. Pages 50 to 52. For starters.

B GEOFF*'s flat. The following morning.*

GEOFF. Were you – raped?

Pause.

FLORENCE. No.

GEOFF. And your family – is anyone – did anyone – survive?

FLORENCE. Some. In exile. The most part.

GEOFF. In camps?

FLORENCE. What – sorry – what is your name?

GEOFF. My name?

FLORENCE. Yes. I did not ask.

GEOFF. Geoff.

FLORENCE. Geoffrey. Can I trust you Geoffrey?

GEOFF. Of course. Of course.

Pause.

FLORENCE. My mother –

GEOFF. The teacher.

FLORENCE. No. She inspected – schools.

GEOFF. Yes of course. She – died?

FLORENCE. No she is alive.

GEOFF. Thank God.

FLORENCE. Yes. God is to be thanked. She is in the Congo.

GEOFF. Right.

FLORENCE. And father is in Kenya and he is very well, he has friends there and he is a skilled man.

GEOFF. They fled then.

FLORENCE. Yes.

GEOFF. Before the killings.

Pause.

Because of the invasion.

FLORENCE. No later they left – later.

GEOFF. And they were, I'm sorry I have to ask this, Kanga, themselves?

FLORENCE. They were Irundi.

GEOFF. Now come on come on what were they, come on let's just be clear, what are you, I mean come on.

Silence.

FLORENCE. Mother was classified as Muntu and father was, although he did not say this often, was a mix. My husband…

GEOFF. Ah you're married too of course.

FLORENCE. No, my fiancé, he's dead, we were engaged to be married but we broke it –

GEOFF. How did he die?

FLORENCE. I don't know. He was killed. Maybe they thought he was Kanga, I don't know, he looked Kanga, he was tall, thin, good looking – I – he was a priest, he preached 'In God there is no Jew or Greek'.

Silence.

Is this what you want to know?

GEOFF. How did you – get out, get here?

FLORENCE. I was in a camp, I translated between the United Nations and Catholic Charities and my commune; my good English helped and the sisters noted my piety and I was lucky enough not to be killed in the camp dispersal –

GEOFF. Yes I read about those – awful –

FLORENCE. The nuns said I was like a dead woman. Six stone. I had dysentry. I felt like my life poured from out of me. I was covered in excrement. They said I was 'un ange, un ange'. That is because they did not know who I was.

GEOFF *looks at her.*

GEOFF. What – what do you mean?

FLORENCE. Please please no more questions please no more –

GEOFF. No no I'm sorry no but you must tell me because you
see I can help you, I see that, but only if I know what they
did to you – Christ, this is what never gets articulated – I
mean it's as if you and your country are not to be permitted
our unique European qualities of – nuance – ambivalence –
no no – talk to me, I think it might be hugely – cathartic
and – I'll write it down – have you written this down – has
anyone – written this –

FLORENCE. It is written inside of me. No one must know.

GEOFF. There's no shame in this – hey – your reserve is
admirable but it plays into the hands of the simplifiers –

FLORENCE. No one must ever know.

GEOFF. Your silence protects the real killers.

FLORENCE. Yes yes it must protect the killers yes –

GEOFF. What?

FLORENCE. I have killed and killed and watched killings and
assisted killings and killers – I have – snatched babies from
mothers and thrown them – I have drawn up lists of names
of those to be exterminated – have ticked lists off of the dead,
checked off against heaps of dead, him, tick, her, tick –

GEOFF. No – no – hang on – no – this is –

FLORENCE. I tell you yes now yes I tell you what I tell no
one – my mother gave beer and food to the killers, welcome
to our home, here my daughter, delighted to meet you,
enchanted, father, here, beers for the workers, thank you
sir, it is hard work there are many many of them, mother,
Florence you will never see *inyenzi* lover again, non
maman, non –

GEOFF. Your mother taught – she was a – teacher –

FLORENCE. Yes yes in schools in colleges the killers walked and killed, the campus, my classes of fellow students – he, he, she there, yes, – denounce – there, there – Felicien, Agathe, Melchior – here their names – their rooms, their streets, their halls – knock on the door with the men with panga, with guns – don't leave yet, check the ceiling, it's false, there hiding, why do you hide, what do you fear, there there – check the latrine, even down in the dirt they hide they wait –

GEOFF. You're being hysterical you –

FLORENCE. And yes yes the children too yes – I ask – what harm are they let us spare the children at least – Father: Do they not grow into men? Mother: Did we not spare them in the past – now they return yes yes – pull out the roots or the weed will grow anew, clear the bush burn the earth, to replant to begin again – even the women with their young unformed in their bellies – split the belly open water bursts out, the seed torn from the gourd – oh oh oh – once you begin, once you start, you must never ever stop, you must never cease to kill, daily, hourly –

She screams. She is suddenly still. Long silence.

GEOFF. Oh – oh –

He slumps to the floor. Silence.

GEOFF. I mean you were – are – you are – what – a christian – aren't you?

FLORENCE. Yes yes – and I will be forgiven, yes, this is my hope, yes. I will confess and I will be forgiven. For Lord from this day on I will never burden you with this again and from that time on I have been without spot or sin and I never hurt another man or woman or child and I will think upon my wrongs and the wrongs done to me and I will forgive –

GEOFF. You will forgive – what?

FLORENCE. The many slights and abuses. And I will obey my mother and my father and will bring them unto safety.

Silence.

GEOFF. I think I've been – labouring under a – terrible – misapprehension –

FLORENCE. Aides moi Geoffrey j'ai peur, j'ai peur.

A GEOFF *and* PAULETTE *and* ALAN. PAULETTE *with the report.*

PAULETTE (*reading*). 'Testimony of a Laurent Gitarama: the commune was assembled by our bourgmestre Jean Kiyabe' (question: How were you called) 'By radio: 'Come come all Muntu people, all families, fathers and sons, come, a matter of great magnitude, we must form a committee of public safety, all come together': we met in the village school –'

ALAN. I believe you taught there.

GEOFF. Yes.

PAULETTE. 'Fifty of us men, some wives, boys also. We were instructed to bring our *pangas* –' what, what's that?

GEOFF. Oh, oh – a sort of machete –

ALAN. What the bloody hell are they all doing with machetes?

GEOFF. What do you think? They work the land. What do you think? Christ. A machete, a tool.

PAULETTE. 'The meeting was exciting. M. Kiyabe spoke to us, words such as 'now we must clear the bush' with 'the righteous anger of the ancient Muntu family' which now would speak in deeds not words – 'You have suffered enough – I have felt your pain, your hunger, your fears, you rise and die in dust and at the same time the *inyenzi* –' what, what is that word I keep coming across it – ?

GEOFF. It means 'cockroach'. Can we stop this, this is futile really.

ALAN. I think the very least you can do is listen in silence.

PAULETTE. 'The next day we assembled in the dawn and beat our way through the *ingo* –'

GEOFF. Village. Well not quite. Plural for *rugo* – homestead.

PAULETTE. 'All Kanga were driven out with shouts and calls and cries. Some were sly and hid in banana groves in the marshes of the lake in the houses of Muntu neighbours but others denounced them, and the roads were blocked and they all all ran to the school – I would say that I myself did not wish to kill, these were my neighbours. But M. Kiyabe had the military men with him, the gendarmes and called out that he would kill any man who did not play his part –'

GEOFF. Please, please, don't don't go on with it, don't keep – just stop stop, point well taken, well fucking –

ALAN. You will listen to the whole thing, the whole of it, yes.

PAULETTE. 'Kill any man who did not play his part. I myself can report that I witnessed M. Kiyabe take a *panga* and kill in one blow a young baby on a woman's back and toss it down like it was garbage and when the woman screamed kill me kill me kill me he instructed me –' (*Pause.*) 'He instructed me to – rape her – and when I replied that I did not wish to he became angry and he – (*Pause.*) – he – struck her in the face with the *panga* and she raised her hands – and he – and she lay – with the – and he was – I was – covered in her – blood' – err – it goes on – not even a third of the way – it goes on – err – 'later in the school so many were now dead that the drains filled with their blood' – p. 35 – p. 46 'our dogs even our dogs fed on those' – then other voices; a survivor – you say you – did you say you – read it? You have criticisms of this? You stupid shit? Yes? Geoff? Do I know you?

ALAN. Paulette.

PAULETTE. I met this man. I kissed this man on his cheeks, bought him a bloody drink.

GEOFF. You don't – know, you don't –

PAULETTE *stands and shakes* GEOFF.

PAULETTE. What's happened to you?

ALAN. Let him think about it.

GEOFF. I don't need to think about – anything.

He stands, takes the report and tears it up.

GEOFF. This is – calumny – and besides even if even if even if there was any degree of truth any even if we sit here in this castle high above the world so high up we can't smell the burning we sit here with paperwork and we make judgements from so very fucking high up from this temple of ignorance –

ALAN. Jesus –

GEOFF. These are awful things yes I don't actually think we are capable of understanding this – are you saying I've known nothing is that what you're saying, that I knowingly what that I knowingly or or otherwise what stood by and allowed people to die people I knew I backed the wrong fucking horse, did this man, you, you met him, you saw this man, his body racked by dysentry you heard him speak this broken reed of a man – this was war, we are thousands of miles away we move paper around in response to paper we sit in bars in rooms we talk to each other in rooms we vote in rooms we consider ourselves ethical, I'm tired of it, to tell the truth I –

Pause.

PAULETTE. I couldn't finish it – I – stopped – too – pathetic –

ALAN. Get out of this building you fucking idiot. You liar.

Pause.

GEOFF. I didn't see the appendices.

PAULETTE. Just full of names.

GEOFF. Names of…

PAULETTE. The dead.

ALAN. You will be utterly discredited. You will be revealed for the bullshitter you are.

GEOFF. I'd like to take a look at that.

PAULETTE. Alan can I have a moment with –

Pause.

ALAN. You sure this is wise.

PAULETTE. I don't care about that.

Pause.

ALAN. I can't guarantee you won't go with him.

PAULETTE. Fine, fine.

ALAN *goes.* GEOFF *leafing through the appendix.*

GEOFF. I wondered if there was a woman. I can't – could you look for me? Who were you reading there?

PAULETTE. Err, someone called – Laurent Gitarama – I think –

GEOFF. Nothing about anyone called – Odette – no, details?

PAULETTE. I don't know. There are so many names here, in an appendix: 'Felix Gitarama, Chantal Muzivungu, Patrice –' pages of them. Look. The dead. Ah, here. Odette. I can't pronounce it. And there. Another one.

He takes the report reads it quietly to himself. She sits. Silence.

Sound of Irundi music. FLORENCE *in towel.* TIM *enters but speaks as* GEOFF.

TIM. This shot shows a woman of the Kanga folk preparing food.

PAULETTE. Nothing can mitigate this, nothing.

TIM. It's hard for us perhaps not to see what we might describe as subjection as what it is, something quite natural.

PAULETTE. Nothing I can imagine. Nothing at all.

Pause.

GEOFF. No.

TIM. This would be a mistake. So, she's not smiling. Well she feels embarrassed having her photograph taken. That's why she's not smiling.

GEOFF. The lake where we swam – the lake where we swam even –

Sound of laughing and swimming. Pause.

Filled with the dead.

FLORENCE *enters, the same space. She and* GEOFF *speak at once.*

GEOFF/FLORENCE. What do I do now?

PAULETTE. You have to start over.

GEOFF (*to* FLORENCE). You have to start again.

FLORENCE. With what I have done?

GEOFF. With what I know?

PAULETTE. Everywhere you can, every opportunity you can you recant recant, on every occasion until you are sick of it.

GEOFF. Yes, tell the truth of it. Some were led, some led, some were willing, some not so, some merely looked on, some waved it on from afar, some knew, some knew and chose to – or knew and couldn't – feel.

Pause. GEOFF *holds* FLORENCE.

GEOFF. I'll get you out. To Canada. I'll get you a flight. To Canada you say? No one will know anything there. There you can be someone utterly new. Where do your family live?

FLORENCE. Montreal.

GEOFF. Good yes, good, go to Montreal and forget – I'll get your papers cleared, I know who we need to see – until you get there and maybe thereafter you are Kanga, yes, Kanga?

GEOFF *holds* FLORENCE; PAULETTE *goes;* TIM/GEOFF *with tape-recorder.*

TIM. I want to play you some music now a tune that some of you probably will think is out of tune. But again that's simply because it is a different scale, a different music, in tune with its own tunes but not with ours. And of course that takes some getting used to. Well, let's just take a listen, shall we.

The music plays; FLORENCE *dances,* GEOFF *hums, the light dims.*

FLORENCE. I am condemned to live.

Blackout.

A Nick Hern Book

World Music first published in Great Britain in 2003
as a paperback original by Nick Hern Books, 14 Larden Road,
London W3 7ST, in association with the Crucible, Sheffield

Typeset by Country Setting, Kingsdown, Kent CT14 8ES
Printed and bound in Great Britain by Bookmarque, Croydon,
Surrey

A CIP catalogue record for this book is available from
the British Library

ISBN 1 85459 762 0